Go From the Night

Poetry

Journeys of Thought
Meditations on Life

Glen Aubrey

www.GoFromTheNight.com
www.CreativeTeamPublishing.com

Creative Team Publishing
San Diego

First Printing

ISBN: 978-0-9797358-1-3
PUBLISHED BY CREATIVE TEAM PUBLISHING
www.CreativeTeamPublishing.com
San Diego

Printed in the United States of America

Go From the Night

Poetry

Journeys of Thought
Meditations on Life

Glen Aubrey

www.GoFromTheNight.com
www.CreativeTeamPublishing.com

Living touches places in imagination's lore
Learning epic lessons of antiquity once more
Refusing what the foolish ones had chosen to respect
Hold onto truths that even fewer ones inspect

Dedication

Go From the Night is dedicated to the adventuresome seeker of truth who is content only with recurring desires for discovery, decision-making, diligent action, dedication to excellence, and the achievements of destiny. He or she thoroughly enjoys the journeys of engagement and invites others of like mind, heart, soul, and expression to join and participate unreservedly in quests that touch the soul and alter life. Joan, this is for you.

Permission

Memory dedication, "In Remembrance of Keith," used by permission of Keith's wife, Colleen Koellish, and their children, Brandon, Taylor, and Shanelle.

Thanks

Piano music manuscript reduction and transcription:
Greatest Song Among Men
There Is a Redeemer
Harvey Tellinghuisen

Editing for Creative Team Publishing:
Jordan Peck

Cover design:
Justin Aubrey

Table of Contents

Genesis 13

Belief 13
Stimulation 17
Expression 21
Business 23

Poetry 29

Accepted 31
Access 33
Acquiescence 35
Alienation 37
Ambiguity 39
Apparition 41
Appeal 43
Attrition 45
Beauty 47
Canvass 49
Certainty 51
Commodities 53
Complexity 55
Confidence 57
Connection 59
Covering 63
Curtain 65
Cylindrical 67
Decision 69

Degrees 71
Depths 73
Distribution 75
Do 77
Echo 79
Effortless 81
Embrace 83
Enrichment 85
Enter 87
Epic 89
Exchange 93
Explanations 95
Factor 97
Fallen 99
Fist 101
Force 103
Foul 105
Gentle 107
Greatest Song Among Men 109
Hear 111
Horizon 113
Hours 117
Image 119
Imbued 121
Inertia 123
Institution 127
Invitation 131
Islands 133
Left 135
Lines 137
Links 139
Match 141
Meal 143
Mechanism 145
Memory 147

Mixtures 149
More 151
Movement 153
One 155
Opening 157
Passion 159
Planted 161
Portion 163
Position 165
Power 167
Presumption 169
Pulse 171
Ready 173
Recorded 175
Reflection 177
Rehearsal 179
Reign 181
Release 183
Remainder 185
Repetitiously 187
Reserve 189
Restitution 191
Reward 193
Secure 195
Senses 197
Shade 199
Shadow 201
Solitude 203
Textures 205
There Is a Redeemer 207
Throb 209
Touch 211
Trees 213
Turned 215
Twenty 217

Two 219
Unquenched 221
Views 223
Vista 225
Warmth 227
Whole 229
Winding 231

Terminus 233

Knowledge 233
Wisdom 234
Action 235
Destiny 236

Greatest Song Among Men music manuscript 239

There Is a Redeemer music manuscript 241

Acknowledgements 243

The Author 247

The Publisher 249

Products 251

Genesis

Belief

Agreements matter. Mysteries surrounding their origins and outworkings await discovery for seriously inquisitive, soulfully inspired, and intellectually diligent adventurers. Sojourners may grow weary from their efforts, but they compromise nothing. They pursue regardless, pressed on by higher motives of fulfilling the lofty goals of learning, living, and loving.

Path-makers are growing ones who, as processes of education and realignment unfold, endeavor to communicate truths with those who make sufficient time and take enough genuine interest to listen beneath the surface of the ordinary. People who engage and cooperate in such engagements are rare. Too often, those who might otherwise give and receive do not agree on even bare essentials (the words they choose, for example), and their journeys may never begin or else end quickly after commencing.

Terms possess meanings that must be discovered and declared. Words like "peace" and "satisfaction" may signify absence of conflict and contentment in one environment and, in alternative circumstances, constitute managed tolerance and severe discomfiture. What a state of peace is for one may be a state of unrest for another. What a state of satisfaction is for one may be a state of repression for another. To ones for whom "peace" and "satisfaction" portray desired and acquired states of being, their conditions can, in different circumstances, bode negative and unwanted conditions for others, regardless of the reasons.

Life-change communication in language, motive, and method occurs when agreements exist regarding the interpretations of words a conversationalist chooses—if he or she wants to understand and be understood. Cooperative terminology and applications are of far more value than the disconnecting points that can divide otherwise interested parties.

Efforts to communicate with disinterested persons constitute needless expenditures of desire and energy. Don't choose to engage in deep interaction with those who are selfishly uninterested, or try to dissuade them from a gross lack of attentiveness, where stimuli may provoke reactions from merely the thinnest layers of their senses. If depth of comprehension and enlightened emotional, mental, and spiritual awareness are goals that drive intentional and rewarding conversations, seek co-laborers.

Educated and expanding perspectives open doors to new understandings and undertakings. Those who dwell in "believing only what I am told" without exercising the due diligence of personal discovery portray ignorance on levels seen at the third grade. Alternative opinions or differing views surrounding any subject are sought and welcomed by people secure enough in their own beliefs to engage in thoughtful and inquiring discussions about others' without the raising of eyebrows and the premature, often inaccurate, judgments and corresponding criticisms originating from preconceived notions, many of which are proven to be incorrect when subjected to more thorough investigation.

A process of attaining maturity never ceases until its living opportunity is closed. Growing up is the conviction and the consequence of seeking people. To achieve their goals, parties on similar paths must covenant to communicate and journey together, only departing from each other's company when agreements on the basics fail. Entering a covenant of understood language, life-cohesiveness, and principle-adherence is not optional if a sojourner desires the companionship of soul mates.

A covenant is an agreement between people who trust each other, have each other's best interests at heart, who embrace similar if not identical values, and who faithfully engage in agreed practices. A moral covenant implies and declares love and desire. The arrangement requires loving obedience—a part of giving and receiving, learning and teaching—sure evidences of heart-felt yearnings to uphold and build upon enduring relationships, where the decisions of one party faithfully regard and earnestly support the other's success.

Trace the actions of a caring person's invasion—with permission—into another human being's space and likely you will discover unrequited love expressed in sacrifice. This sacrifice proves that when one says "I love you," the words include the intentional giving away of some things of supreme value for the good of the ones who are destined to receive the benefits. Apart from this offering, a covenant may be words only, void of proofs.

A worldview that includes listening to the views of another (whether or not initial agreement exists), submission to agreed tenets (where this interconnectivity is possible), and willful sacrifice to broaden and encourage another person's journey of discovery points to development of a covenant in process. Beginning one requires joining with persons who want to grow and mature with you, people who, because of this connection, may be willing to pursue roads of discovery heretofore not realized, though perhaps dreamt.

Pro-activity and response follow higher calls of obedience to history's proofs, where values that endure beyond temporary tests become ties that bind parties within their quests, freed from chronicled and prison-caged vacuums of understanding and associated examples of unwillingness to investigate. Covenants adhered in principle are agreements revered in respect. These are demonstrated in practical living—through an individual's experiences and within those of the people whose lives are touched.

You and fellow-responders in cooperative endeavors generate positive and enduring legacies when you build upon what you agree. Don't try to contribute and live within what you don't. Belief in and action upon mutual and unalterable agreements constitute elements of constructing enduring covenants on which you can count and to which you can and should contribute.

Truth-borne covenants are rare because the walls that prevent interchange are often higher than the desires to construct roads of communication that allow and promote open and uplifting connectivity. Clearly, these walls must be torn down where the goals to promote growth of God-inspired qualities of life and liberty are more important than the negative status quo, where people are violated, devalued, demeaned, and destroyed.

The responsibility of the earnest learner is to reach beyond the norm and seek the form that best positions seekers to expand learning, respect character, and verify truth in objective analysis, appealing to emotions through absolutes, not in manufacturing excuses for abiding in their absence.

To capture in poetic word the full depths of profound promises of belief and practice shall remain an unending quest. But *Go From the Night* states emphatically that those who seek with all their might will be given sharpened sight—

glimpses and revelations of the profound truth and endurance of this maxim: Covenant makers keep their word because words and works are connected and uphold one another, else there is no covenant.

Believing, affirming, and fulfilling tenets of revealed, developing, and maturing covenant relationships give life. These are the time-honored truths taught and celebrated within this book.

Agreements matter. Honor yours.

Stimulation

The length and breadth of one's attention span may be seen in the degrees of internal or external stimulation required to hold his or her interest. Stimuli, regardless of sources, affect us all. To what stimuli do you respond and why? What are your touch points?

Life's phases and stations attract, retain, and repel stimuli. Awareness of emotion, spirituality, physical wellbeing or disease, senses of hearing, touch, smell, sight, taste, character of the core, ingenuity, creativity, belief systems, and intelligence are grids through which stimulation must pass if it is to make a mark on its subject.

Consider: What do you not hear when you and your world are silent? How often do you practice a presence of solitude? What sights bid you stop and wonder at creation's majesty? What music moves you to greater depths of meaning and profound wonder? What spiritual expressions reach deepest into your soul? What sources of stimulation cause you to laugh, cry, sing, become angry, forgive, or firmly decide fresh courses of action? What principles of your worldview are unalterable regardless of the stimuli you receive? From what sources do you receive information that positions you to decide which truths are immovable? How sensitive are you to unfamiliar cultural stimuli? What sources of multi-cultural input have you experienced? How eager are you to expand receptivity to the stimuli of cultures you do not know? What controls do you desire or possess that focus stimulation toward preferable or desired objectives? What controls prevent you from investigating stimuli that are foreign to you?

Who are the messengers to whom you pay rapt attention and why? Reflect on the content and urgency of their messages. Consider how their methods of communication affect your receptivity. Receivers who want to gain and retain all they can from the stimuli that most affect them assure that truths of important messages are not obscured by a messenger's idiosyncrasies, including (but not limited to) insufficient knowledge, lack of efficient and effective styles, differing languages, misunderstood expressions, or negative behaviors perhaps born of ignorance and not birthed by design.

Where the message and the messenger are cohesive in intent and contribute to comprehension and positive impact, the earnest and maturing receiver takes and sifts both, carefully weighing the effectiveness of each. Indeed, where motives adhere to eternal standards, truth-telling can be present regardless of style, in thoughtfully conceived expression that is purposefully offered. Truth should be willingly embraced no matter its form of presentation.

Think of people, sources of education, and communication media that have truly moved you. Who and what were they, and what are the life-lessons you received from them? If you have expressed your gratitude to people who have stimulated you, be congratulated for right action. If you have not and still can, when will you? Positive simulation should never be underestimated or taken for granted. It should be treasured and affirmed as are the people who have inspired you nobly honored.

Interruptions to productive stimuli are imposters when they dissuade learning. Their disguises are many. Mindless noise may be a source of angst and disruption—what are its sources? Rudeness may be a characteristic of conversations you should not tolerate. Blatant disregard for mutual understanding and inherent or generated vacuums of respect are other intruders to, and inhibitors of, creative stimuli.

What are the blockades to your creative and engaged thinking? How do you handle meaningless cacophonies and invasive distractions? Of what value is quiet solitude when your deep thinking requires stillness and how dedicated are you to protect and enhance it?

In consideration of your working environments, what stimuli promote your best efforts at accomplishing required goals? How important are projects or prerequisite obligations to which you must be committed in order to live? Are they merely tolerated or purposefully and creatively embraced? What effects do your attitudes and approaches produce on deliverables that require your creativity and accountability?

Pain, of course, is another stimulus. Pain moves its recipients to avoidance, conflict, healing methodologies, changes of environment, or mixtures of these. Handling pain appropriately constitutes actions born of developing maturity. Causing pain willfully to the degradation of another is evil. Allowing pain to control you is choosing to live within its damaging effects when you possess the response-ability to choose otherwise.

Pain inflicted from without or within bears rooted causes. Dealing with pain at beneficial, long-lasting, relief-generating, and healing levels demonstrates an understanding of sources to chart best courses to confront, avoid, or conquer its discomforts, but in all cases to endeavor not to be controlled by it.

What is desired, and may be required, is the developing knowledge of the stimulators that touch you most and why, as well as your choices of response. Shy away from or simply refuse those that confuse or foment destructive engagements. You must decide preferred patterns in which positive decision-making can occur, patterns that encourage maximum learning and best judgment.

Poetry, regardless of style, may be one of several welcomed means of truth receptivity for you. If so, ask: What styles best suit your learning? How willing are you to investigate alternative communication modes and methods if it could be shown that receptivity to knowledge and wisdom is heightened? How would you discover your best choices apart from investigation?

Further, consider: Who might learn from your preferred ways of communication as both a receiver and giver? How willing are you to create noticeably fresh stimuli for those to whom you wish to communicate? The models of receptivity for one may not be the standards of receiving for another. Wisdom seeks to know the differences and to choose the most effective ones for application. How much do you desire to be a source of stimulation? Whether desired or not, you are.

Go From the Night is a collection of poetic stimulation. Perhaps some of the selections will move you to contemplation and, upon in-depth consideration and evaluation, motivate you to engage in purposed action born of changed desires and designs. Regardless, you will observe and retain more if you decide what needful stimuli to embrace and what to shun as you turn the pages and think.

Expression

Producing art is a consumptive task, required by anyone who learns, applies, and expresses art-stimulated interchanges of ideas, regardless of form. The process is rewarding and contributory when theme, timing, target, and treasure are recognized by author and audiences for the ways in which they connect.

Your life has themes—intermeshed views, vistas, vicissitudes, victimizations, and victories. Learning from their content, comprehending how they form and mold you, and choosing to embrace and communicate their living proofs are lifelong engagements, whether or not you choose art as a means to express them.

Included in your themes are recurring patterns of involvement in other's lives, recently discovered information, collections of experiences, education, and environments—some chosen for you and, as maturity occurs, those chosen by you. Receiving truth from all of them requires openness of mind and heart, as well as the formation of grids of belief against which their values and merits must be weighed.

Gratitude leads the list of expressive actions that recognize and validate the worth of the themes of your life. Learning from mistakes as well as meritorious achievements, and being appreciative of them, shows balance in the classrooms of living.

For what and to whom are you thankful? How often do you voice your gratitude to those whose contributions have enriched your life, known by them or not, whether achieved through negative or positive circumstances? What procedures do you thoughtfully employ to communicate appreciation to others? If your expressiveness does not include proactive thanksgiving remember: To the degree you are thankful is the degree to which you are able to receive thanksgiving and appreciation from others.

Thanksgiving is a vital part of living holistically. Participating in it requires no other agenda than expressing humility for gifts others have presented to you. Offering thanksgiving and praise freely from sincere desires to build up, encourage, and align with good principles and practices are parts of the processes of maturing. Immature and selfish individuals are reticent to give praise because they are too insecure to receive it.

Beyond thanksgiving—its actions and shared benefits—what other means of expression do you choose and who are your audiences? For anyone who seeks strong, enduring, and positive relationships, the motive of the heart becomes and remains serving your networks for the sake of the good that your investments generate within them and you.

Modes of expression are many, perhaps innumerable. All originate from core desires and are seen in observable actions. Examples may be evidenced in numerous fields of endeavor. Among them are the arts, sports, construction, interior decorating, intentional acts of mercy and forbearance, cooking, hospitality, caring for the elderly or infirm, teaching, leading, following accountably by giving your best to your company or enterprise, balancing work with rest, interpreting for the deaf, attending games of the teams you support, participating enthusiastically in group efforts of teams on which you serve, financially contributing to worthy causes, policing, engaging in government for the public good, fighting fires, protecting loved ones, engaging militarily for God and country, upholding principle in trying circumstances, loving, truth-telling, being a peace-maker, forgiving wrongs within others and yourself, exercising patience with those whose behaviors test it, being a good patient of the ones who care for you, respecting others for who they are, righting wrongs appropriately, controlling yourself, offering and providing assistance especially behind the scenes, restoring relationships and building new ones—the list is endless.

Go From the Night asks you to express yourself, and to do so for your good and that of others by creating environments contributory to growth. Choices of expressions may move you to consider changing some of your behaviors. You may be challenged to wonder, consider, and perhaps act on difficult decisions for best results. You will cherish some of these choices, and others will be uncomfortable. You may consider viewing and treating your networks, circles of impact, influence, and investment, and yourself differently.

How willing are you to engage in making you and your world better? Improving your environments is not optional when you desire to live, contribute, and receive holistically. Begin with a focus on what you can give because of what you desire to leave as a legacy. Express what you want *from* others through contributing *to* them initially. Continue and *never give up*.

You will illustrate the rule of rules whose golden truths have preceded us and will last beyond our existence, marking time with eternity. Improvements to any environment are not accidental—they demand aspiration, inspiration, and perspiration from those who do more than wish circumstances would get better.

Business

Business is a state of service interaction, product provision, and payment, where methods born of ethical considerations and right actions produce better people and improved products, in that order. Evaluate your business contributions in light of this truth. How do they measure up?

Belief, stimulation, and expression impact your choices of actions that generate wealth. Investigation of business practices of acquiring possessions nearly always includes answering the "How" questions of accumulation.

Ethical business acts upon this principle: Acquire all you can, in all the legitimate ways you can, to retain all you can, to give away all you can, to invest all you can. Your responsibilities are to live within and contribute to the process, continuing this cycle indefinitely.

Inherent in right business practices are obligations to pay what is needful and required to those to whom compensation is due. Recipients include those who work for you, those who provide services and products, those with whom you have business arrangements that obligate you, and those with positions over you whose responsibilities include collecting a part of your income and purchasing power in taxation.

The challenge is to maintain and grow wealth to levels that empower you to distribute portions of it to those you love and care for in this life, and to leave assets for distribution following your death. No one takes personal possessions with them beyond the grave. Assets remain from the efforts one has made while living, last for a time after they are gone, and say much about the returns from expended time and energy. Residual effects are sure and live in the memories of those left behind.

Legacies are born when truths of business practices come to light: how what was acquired was obtained, how services provided matched income received, how debt was handled, and how the worth of the assets was sustained and expanded beyond the initial costs required for accumulating them.

Acquired resources may include money and the tangibles it purchases as well as the intangibles of goodwill, hope, assurance, trust, and other positive characteristics of a giving individual.

Investments are made in people and possessions. In all cases, a worthwhile investment is made where potential returns equate to amounts greater than the original, whose payment is anticipated and proven over time.

Business is a state of profit-generating activity where establishing and building upon foundations of lasting returns can and should occur. Several solid action steps promote sustainable wealth for business people who desire to produce positive legacy. Among them:

1. Pay yourself. Charge enough for your endeavors to realize a profit on every transaction. Fully disclose these amounts where necessary.
2. Pay others more than they expect. Providing a little more than what is anticipated or required goes a long way toward thanking people who are helping you succeed. Assure that the budgets you oversee or to which you contribute allow this activity.
3. Pay the taxes you owe.
4. Use the "10-10-10-70 Percent Allocation" for income: 10% is yours to contribute, 10% is yours to invest, 10% is yours to retain as contingency, and 70% is yours to use to pay the costs of living. Live slightly beneath your means.
5. Donate to causes you can verify and which match your heart's desires to help others.
6. Invest in growing assets; spend less on depreciating ones.
7. Consider the kinds of debt you should acquire, if any. Debt that is leveraged to grow assets can contribute over

time to expanding and sustainable wealth if managed appropriately.

8. Invest in appreciating assets early and continue this activity throughout your life.
9. Legally protect assets for those you love.
10. Give freely to charity and as anonymously as possible.
11. Remember that the costs of achieving greatness, measured on meritorious function, are small compared to the losses resulting from disreputable behaviors that damage and destroy people, their possessions, and reputations.
12. Build people before production. They will produce more as they grow, as will you.

While *Go From the Night* is not a book about business, it is a book about integrated principles of struggle and victory, strengths desired and required in overcoming odds, contributing more for yourself and on behalf of others, and remaking your environments to achieve worthwhile and improved goals, not living in insufficiency, negativism, undue criticisms, and worthless consequences. Changing negative conditions to positive ones will impact and hopefully improve your personal life experiences as well as your workplace contributions.

Please see the following websites for business, leadership, and team development books by Glen Aubrey:
> *www.LeadershipIs.com*
> *www.IndustrialStrengthSolutions.com*
> *www.CoreTeamsWork.com*
> *www.Lead52.com*

Go From the Night speaks to instituting and dwelling in holistic, integrated, and improving engagements. No internal decisions exist without eventual external proofs. If the improvements you earnestly desire in personal and business dealings are those for which you firmly decide to expend necessary energies to make them come true, your rewards are sure—whether in this life or the next.

What you hold as beliefs, the stimuli to which you respond, your willful expressions, and business practices tell much about your willingness to stay where you are or change what needs to be improved if improvement is truly desired. What you learn and the wisdom to apply it determine your destiny and will leave a legacy for those who follow.

Central questions are: What are your longings for life change? How much do you want them? When will you go from nights of discouragement and insufficiency into revealed lights of expanding opportunity? You begin a living process and follow it through to term when you earnestly desire to achieve positive and residual effects—for yourself and those about whom you care deeply.

Poetry

Accepted

In, cased, centered, secured, assured, purposed, grappling,
    grasped, enfolded, leased, draped, and leaned,
    Retained folds,
    Warm.

Quintessence of medieval lore lures calmed flavors'
metamorphoses.
    Columns, aligned, raise their masts; secretive natures
    display primal forms.
    Disquietude falls in timed, tiered truth, telling all.

Darkened moons lift vassals while prominence's unrevealed
worlds are shown;
    Brightened, softer sceneries
    Speak of misty voyages.

How must coarse insensitivities not reach to try to asphyxiate
    august experiences?

Vanity's efforts, fruitless and azure hues' palatial spaces, dusty,
allure.
    Rejection's prominences bend rigidity's staunch
    prerequisites,
    Shouting insults that wrench timidity from its bounds.

Longevity passes a stillness surpassed by moistened tones.
    Glistening memories linger.
    Embedded horizons fade, are fed, then freed, are
    reborn.

Mysteries permeate stilled spaces.
    Abatements quiet streams.
    Flows know familiar insecurities and paced effects issue
naught.

Fun, that ancient truth teller, hides mid fogs that shroud truer
intents.
    Germinating, although paused momentarily, treasured
    secrets, like crustaceans, breed.
    They will a coming, in timed cadence.

In store, fully stocked and stoked, starvation ceases while
living, achieved, rises, reigns, and rules in places forbidden only
yesteryear.

    Joyful choruses bless this country's new forms, fenced
    no longer, held captive nevermore.
    Moaning, milling, and meandering, the meaninglessness,
    forbidden, fades.

Access

Permissions unpaid, not brought nor bought,
But by forces
        Themselves parties of impure essence
        Of one whose belligerence shuts and seals doors,

Boxed in, closed, incommunicado, cloistered, claustrophobic;
these cold isolations stiffen in their resistance toward any who
dare approach.

Why this loneliness? There is no communication.

        Silenced, a vacuum shrieks to be heard,
        Yearning to listen
        Though reception is faint.

Open a door, wreath-adorned and welcoming.

Acquiescence

Becoming crude, disparaging, thick, and crippled, the hoped-
for satisfactions from distanced and charming views never
materialized.
    Carried as approaching vacations into storms of reality,
    their willingness cowered when thin and tiny coverings
    were unceremoniously removed.
    Essential separations marked all-too frequent
    confrontations when issues of the commonplace shoved
    aside fantasies of history and desire.

What is good for one may not be good for another; it seldom is.
    Stretched beyond abilities to grasp, the straightened
    is bent as newer muscles impose strange and unfamiliar
    twists upon the disheartened and lonely.
    Ease has vanished, relinquishing its open hands,
    spreading palms as though waving through grain, but only
    dregs remain from this shorn harvest.

Incurrence takes all forms; incursion, its birth mother, usually less.
    Leisure's commands are unfulfilled plans, relaxation flows
    only where tastes for truths are similar, if not identical—
    what futile hope this too often is.
    Strewn hastily about, stringent ties constrict youngsters'
    souls, constructing life and death prisons for any who'd
    flee.

Quenched, panted voices—dilapidated and oh, so tired of the
dirge—beg for refreshment amid dry lands, but water is nowhere.
    Sculpted models, devoid of life, answer back nothing.
    Formatted, aligned, conformed, standing free,
    Dumb to the world, they see, hear, and feel not.

Rogues intrude on these scenes at night and, with a vigilance of heroism, awaken and loose the captives, to try to let them go.

Barring death they may succeed if the eyes, ears, and limbs of the captured and released ones hearken to and obey fresh commands, though at the time grossly misunderstood and barely trusted.

The guards, embarrassed, discover gaping holes in their own abutments and, after the fact, are forbidden to share their morose and failure-ridden countenances; rather, they are commanded to seek hidden places to shelter their scorn— like cockroaches cowering under dirty carpeting.

Alienation

Though separated, two or more may join irreconcilable views
and mold reachable friendships, intertwined and understood.

Impressionable reasoning desires fate's destined truthfulness.
    Before its time it danced on narrow terraces of
    consequence
    Then removed itself to hidden matrices to form anew.

Remembrance pervades and makes precious its recovery.
    A new and neutral birth is a life to meld.

Search the records and turnstiles.
    Turn styles and substances into wholesome and softer
    beauties.

Questions are unmasked and affirmation answers.
    Familiar responses from genuine hearts become
    welcomed dwellings.

Sub-matter relishes its attention-grabbing.
    Conscious tears dry on cold stones,
    Their avenues buried, reduced to planes, depths, and
    simpler constitutions.

Health breaks its quietude, calling in contrition
    To the person who endeavors to fulfill her promises.

Competing interests though shorn of barbs, share no common
place.

Ambiguity

Ambition pawns its soul and pauses to check why.
 A mid-course, coarse correction,
 A run, strung over shards
 Requires calloused feet if bleeding is to be prevented.

These unshapen paths are bald before the sun;
 Shade, through relentless and careless harvesting,
 Has long since withdrawn.
 It will not come again in this life.

When the dawn breaks the ambiguous night will cease.
 Expectant rays, formerly masked by a simpleton's
 threats, will obliterate the blight.

Critical hate, ambition thwarted, is placed on yet another shelf
of indisposition, disinclining its distain for another day, if it
comes.
 No matter, it will come.

Resurrect health.
 Look, seek, crave, and embrace.
 Break, and mend the mind and soul.

Solely set another course.
 Coerced minds cannot follow, nor should they.
 A purer song is still yours.

Apparition

Under-covered, tin-sheltered, corrugated cardboard treasures mistaken for rubbish, reside in isolation, unnoticed, though desperate to distribute their wealth.

Self-centeredness and abandoned grief mix.
    Formed from offscreen relief and unseen belief
    Impulse's non-productive characters
    Revel in stark apparitions.

A furrowed brow besmirches overwhelming mental anguish.
    Soulfully the sirens wail but there are none who hear,
    care, or even twitch.

Non-repetitive creativity is doomed to vacant halls.

Time is a frame in which cogitated and energized reflections beam if the uncontrolled silence deepens.
    Bodies, unionized, enduring and built to withstand all,
    Risk breaking through the useless fastidious confines,
    Discontent with discontent.

Sick, a tried and tired spot is refreshed when momentum pierces mediocrity.
    For those who frown, the descending and
    de-accelerating varieties of encroachment's vicissitudes
    no longer compete for an environmentalist's ruse.

Depth-charged, plumbed, and bursting with life, the dreamer fears no longer.
    Yielding to beauty, as a treasure that he or she musters
    from the muck, hope is remembered and truth pervades
    the soul.

Resolved: to appear boldly in full regalia for the apparition's demise.
The destined battle toward demurring is fought and won.
The future is secure.

Appeal

Lessening ills, distilling and bearing timeless love, laughter wells
up from the lowest regions, encircling, rolling, surrounding, and
enveloping the matters, displacing pain.

Exchanging the past for peace, it silences stuttering, dispels
rude disturbances, and soothes the mind.

It rejects repetitious lies, aligning with steps of new cadences,
refreshingly energized.
    Peering intently, it grasps salvation and will not let go.

Awakened, a song of strength revives itself as though it had
never departed.
    Graciously it receives assistance and praise.
    Building on its endurance it is emboldened by another's
embrace.

Calling, some answer.
    Those who do, respond with joy.

Attrition

Quests alter life, reveal character, and require choosing.
    Dreamers' desires foment initiatives rare in quality,
    savored in occurrence.
    Revived, wearied ones recall serene benefits of
    uninterrupted rest.
Combined and strengthened, protection assures the senses of
security.
    Gratified, these resume set-aside long-planned
    preparations.

Candid understandings pursue input from diverse sources,
longing for answers.
    Few meaningful ones become known.
    Those that endure, against formidable odds, refresh
    their own kind.
A worth of wealth may not equal the efforts to acquire it.
    Most fail, several succeed, fewer lead.

Chance optimists fade.
    Changed agents, toughened, invite others to come.
    Childish antics revel in the expected and reveal certain
    destinies.
Seldom do major alterations occur apart from imposed
structures.
    These are formed from within and without.

Reserves of the prepared ones move the hungry to eat and the
thirsty to drink.
    These bid the trifling travelers finish their half-run
    courses.
    Mythologies melt on heated surfaces of proof.
Who remains standing?
    In what condition shall they present themselves?

At once unclouded and regal in brightened and blinding lights,
the peaks formerly unknown penetrate the landscapes of
the eyes, mind, and soul, and demand gratified and singular
attention—yours.
       Only imagine what could be!
       Advice from fools predicts their own destruction.
Moan the fallen, but not too long.
       There is work to do.

Affectation precedes futile and shallow admiration.
       Mourning's phrases mumble layered half-truths.
       Sickened senses try to endure what they must until
       eternal rhythms squelch weaker intrusions.
Not all standardized forms fit into prepared containers.
       Needing to be freed, uncommonality requests its own
       champion.

Beauty

An inquisitive imagination refuses sleep when pretentious tranquility is consumed by consciousness.
>Floating stories unfold across the mind.

Their telling reveals strange juxtapositions of longing and loss, life and death.
>Too soon departed, victims of forgetfulness or of false interpretation, thoughts may seldom be completed and must eventually cease.

Pervasive are their inhibitors.
>Interruptions are divestitures of reality and, while perhaps not unbelievable, they are intrusive still.
>Lingering sadness may soon dissolve into momentary memory within interpretations rarely grasped.

Optimal understanding inhibits aimless meanderings when messages and motives again combine.
>Coalescence ushers in great comprehension and attending apprehension.
>The sacred banishes severance.
>The ties are strong that bind.
>They blind as well.

Spiderweb-thin lines build strong bridges when they connect desire with truth.
>Walk balanced, run if you must.
>The mid-point is the beginning of destiny.

An eternal source of fulfillment is yours to attain.

It is reachable. Retrieve it and live. Beauty returns!

Canvass

Youthful indulgence tries to cover uncontrollable drifting.
    Mid wandering reflections,
    Multidirectional beams pierce mists of shaded groves.
    Modules, drooping canopies, liltingly sweep away the
    wayward,
    Leaning, unchanged,
    Tied tightly to closed graves and their engrossing
    thoughts.
    Stillness descends, features molt, casting needlessness
    aside.
        Solitude's respites prerequisite the required.
        Cured, fragile droplets quiver, positioning
        themselves as tiny sentinels against coming and
        foreboding storms.

Anxiety and remorse cling to each other, alone.
    Stymied by infatuation and spread along unending
    paths, they simulate denial's wavering and wilting glances.

Originating from ancient ceremonies, the igniting torchlight
bearers present offerings, lingering, as if by design, until they are
consumed.
    Warring against weariness, distant voices mingle in
    merriment, oblivious to the obvious.

Masquerades unwittingly emit alternative and desperate, fatal
sounds.
    "The torch bearers are gone!"
    "The torch bearers are gone!"
    "Replenish stark voids!"

Repetition, a symbol of remonstration's errors, floods the mighty
causeways.
      Laughter, un-captured, is not free; rather, repressed.
        Sullen and stored away, apart from distant ears,
        simpler movements call.
        Deftly the soul's inward drives tease, teach, and
        tantalize sheer and sheen desires.

Canvassed canopies endure until the sun's rays redirect their
survivors' views.
      Hues, out of alignment, disturb the points, unsettling the
      unexpected.
      Disquieting ambiance consumes natural graces.

Underneath, the lanterns whimper,
      "Too little, too late; too long the wait."
      "Too little, too late; too long the wait."

Latent effects watch, wane, and war.
      They wear upon the worried.
      Lifeless forms from newer realities swim in their own fears.

Ravenous are the appetites of those who don't care.
      They mock those who of their own accords persevere.
      Drawn inexplicably, the ancient rituals' peace mantras
      try and try again to breathe while bound to their own
      despairing experiences.

Another canopy rises, but only for awhile.

Certainty

"I am quite content to know only today," bemoans the fool.
    Greater people possess insatiable quests for knowledge
    of hidden truths,
    Elements contemporaneously unknown.

    "Of tomorrow I'm not sure. My future rest is insecure."

Folly!

The fatalistic drifter's fires are fanned too frequently by ill-
conceived fuels of malcontents.
    Stay away from them, you must.
    You deserve better than all they offer!

Purer notions rest in motions of the sun and stars, the planets
and moon.
    These are sure for as long as you shall live, celestial
    bodies, all.

Best-placed thoughts struggle to subject themselves to
sacrificial monuments, the non-living, non-caring, and non-giving
stones,
    Whose silence, shattered by noncompliance and sheer,
    Unadulterated rebellion, grows unabated.
    Screams of prisoners masked and chained
    Hearken to those whose courage falters
    In expressions of the heart, soul, mind, spirit, and flesh.

    None other than The Interested listen intentionally to
    the groaning travails of The Silenced, and the pains of
    The Suppressed.

They sing a new song of their own composition.
Relieving, grieving, and grateful melodies, capped from
eons of slavery, are released!
They soar in new throats breathing fresher air.

Decry the momentous lamentations no longer.

Now is your opportunity.
Destiny calls.
Answer to chance and change a lifetime.

Secure and well-founded positions no one immediately
can declare.
Forgive the past!
Forge a path!
Brave the brutish unknowns.
Conquer the ravaging scoundrels!
Brace as well for the denials
You know are sure to come.

You may win in the winds of the end.
A long road, this.

Commodities

Blackened strips grace peaceful, flowing, and whitened sands,
    Rebuffed no longer even though
    Rebellious feuds and fences remain, as does hope.

Tailored winds push tethered poles to their touching points.
    Climbing, they clamor to release purer songs,
    Every time.

Rolled, enshrined edifices' cannons are silent tonight.
    Rushing tidal pools return again, and again.
    They endure beyond tumultuous destruction.

Excoriated, those who sought to help seek help from the
helpless.
    Suns rise and fall.
    They rise and fall.

Blurred and vicious visions remain mysteriously clouded.
    Softer sounds diminish hardened, guttural utterances.
    These are voices whose desecrations descry their dread.

Vibrations have foretold these undercurrents.
    Long ago the bountiful beauties had turned to kiss the
prone.
    Their wagers won them nothing.

Renewals, as realignments, form.
    They gather against overwhelming odds.
    They follow grander designs.

For sale, for selling, for buying, foretelling,
    They achieve a cyclical and eternal
    Predominance.

As far as Thee,
      I cannot see.
      Unending efforts' labors oppose unrealized maturity.

When gentle winds grant comfort to weary ones,
      The rest is sweet and sure.

Complexity

The challenge is how to face it.
    Confronted, an opportunity exists
    To move through, conquer, learn, and live.

Destiny frames its characters, those who through former days
imagined they were their own masters.
    Surely the meek inherit the soil and its soiled remains.
    But they are better for it.

Causes carve unknown paths for those who yearn for more.
    A simpleton's revelry entertains multiple audiences
    throughout a myriad of exchanges.
    Tiers and tears bring balance, somehow.

Dropped by degrees with insufficient excuses, the weak seek to
shift responsibility and refuse to shoulder culpability, creativity,
or craft.
    Decisions come; derisions grow.
    After-the-fact gossipers rend their speakers then shred
    them.

True opinions come to light as do motives.
    From what source do covert betrayals come?
    Ah, these confound confluence.

There are no contrite hearts here.
    Compelled as a river toward a falls, momentum takes
    over.
    The unfortunates are swept away by currents of their
    own creation.

Construct dams.
     Build bridges.
     Craft causeways.

The workers, who would accomplish great feats,
     Strain and gasp for breath as oncoming and enveloping
     tides surround them.
     Desires remain but efforts refrain.

Sing songs to the deafened, detached, and numbed.
     Numbered with the heartless and the un-brave, they race
     toward an abyss they previously have known too well,
     A fate their own heads and hands have forged.

Confidence

Why entrust the master controls to ones with furtive and
piercing glances of stealth?
    Drooping eyelids reveal shadowed evil's inclinations.
    Who knows their hearts?
    They yet have hands to play.
    Ploys frolic, though masked in frequent stares,
    Where no one knows devices or ends with surety.

        Lessen the burdens, loosen the chains.
       Fervent, imprisoned ones' constant refrains
      Ring through dank hallways, filling their rooms,
     Pleading for help from the depths of their tombs.

Not so long ago the tables were turned.
    The guns faced the enemy, away from the friends.
    The timing was perfect.
    Predictable ends
    Feigned their allegiance and flaunted their clout;
    When, brutally captured, they fell into doubt.

While strong men supplied their protection, so-called,
    Others in dungeons were conquered and crawled.
    Behind prison bars, freedom's memory passed
    From one who had lived it to one who's die, cast,
    Compelled him to waver enough to be last;
    And last ones are first ones to enter their past.

Be wary the prophet who foretells futures for all but himself.
    He it is who tantalizes the weary,
    Predicting dire destinies
    From gilded and heavily guarded towers.

    Many there are who tell tall tales
    Before they are silenced permanently.

Folly and servitude reign therein.
    The "what could have been" line
    Is the mark of the end line,
    The sentence completed
    Not by one
    Who began it.

A race for the story's conclusion is gore to the ones stripped of hope.
    Passions of flurry dissolve onto pages
    Bearing no remaining stains from a printer's ink wells,
    Where words are neither composed nor completed.
    They are mere blotches
    With hidden meanings.

Connection

Misdirected, the mentally forlorn wanting of fortunes beg for esteem.
>Vicious winds disrupt their meditative bliss,
>Sweeping it away.

Each is dependent on equivalent energy sources, forces with which to be reckoned.
>All related, though severed and broken in their transmissions,
>They unburden themselves at merely hinted provocations.

>>What moves grand seas by small degrees?
>>Do self-contented, earnest pleas?
>>Each desperate ploy plays havoc's games,
>>And in its courses, ruins names.

Misguided, stumbling o'er rocky shoals, a watery edge testifies to Nature's endurance.

>The dead, still breathing
>>To the living,
>>>Seethe with urges,
>>>>Haunting, giving,
>>>>>Resigned to ultimate destinies,
>>>>>>But somehow emboldened, unwilling to go.

Tales of longevity
    Contrast with fables
      Of the feeble
        Who line the shores,
          Rotting,
            Their futures cut short.
           History's refrains
             Eventually cover
               Memory's cords.

Basking in fun, sharing identical enterprises at singular but
different moments, these birthed their own adventures.
    Where one lived on, the second paid the cost, and lost,
    Smothered by continuums of life in which all partake,
    willing or not.

Misunderstandings established their rhythms,
    Unceasing in their cycles of turnings and tumults.
    Triumphant but weather-beaten and older now,

The disconnected ones ventured forth,
    Wandering toward destinations
    Of their own making and undertaking.

What draws aficionados toward systems that may consume
them?
    Have they no understanding
    Or more than the rest?

Sacred artifacts, willfully sacrificed as desperate ones lunge for
learning,
    Plunge,
    Their waters of imagination flowing, unimpeded.

      Let them.

Expunged, microorganisms breed instability and drown
When the living ones shun the dying,
Succumbing to The Inevitable.

61

Covering

Unmasked, shadowed fortune is revealed as pens imprint
papyrus layers.
        Blackened, oblique in spiraling darkness,
        Writers turn scrawls into tall tales.

Unwavering, just remonstrations chronicle desperate scenes,
        Longing to turn them into stories of conquest.
        Leave them alone.

Fashion the door and its chiming bell.
        Both living and dying
        Have stories to tell.

Unfeigned, an egress portrays a new birth.
        Go there from here.
        Re-enter your earth.

                Go from the night.

Voids and vacuums, absent accounts,
        Held bitter-sweet against armored breasts,
        Released to die nobly, and in violent tests
        Arise like the Phoenix from ashes reborn
        To win grandeur, battles, upon a new morn.

When weights are shed and burdens shared,
        The bruised shall live again.
        A difficult road traversed
        Is in itself an end.

Curtain

We would throw them away, if we could.
    Shielding the undesirable,
    They haunt the re-occurring.

Time dictates tattered curtains be taken down, burned, or cut
up for other uses.
    A difficult task, this.
    These folds horde fiber and verve in permanent
    creases,
        Remembered in cascading and unfailing truths,
        Expressions for which
            Audiences paid substantial sums in quests for
            entertainment.

An era is finite.
    When it is through its curtains are drawn tight—
    Conclusive passages are not revisited.

Burst forth from the veil.
    Rend it permanently.
    Usher in new crowds.
        Quote better scripts.
            Present the profession's masterful image.
            Thrill the attendees.

Audiences, captivated, applaud and dance, free of inhibition.
    Learners rush the floodlights,
    Glaring at revelations never beheld.

Stumbling, they are drawn
    As steel to magnets.
    Regaining composure,
      The collected
        Fashion looms
          To sew new curtains
            In formerly familiar venues.

Dazzling no longer, the being behind her fabric coverings is
revealed for what she really is.
    One eternal minute has yielded
    A lifetime of truth.

Threads, thick with blood from torn sinews,
    Lay in heaps upon the ground.
    Who retrieves and discards the old lines?
      Stronger compositions—
        Fabrics sewn of new material—
          Are required to adorn your stage.

The essence of you creates patterns and forces of the knots
you kneed.
    No more ritual and redundant excuses:
    Destiny commands your curtains be drawn when they
    must.

Increase your resolve.

Cylindrical

Blossom's shapes, fashioned from their energies, synergize
communion.
    Though sources remain masked, those who analyze form and
function, marvel.
        Systems, comprehended superficially by so-called
experts,
            Those teachers of less truth than learners of olden
ways,
                Fail in their efforts to promote theory as fact.

Qualifications, influencing and instructing copious crowds,
    Combine neither knowledge nor wisdom.
        Skins recall microscopic beginnings:
            Sheer manipulation, heady stimulation,
                Impressive conversations without systemic
substance.

Shameful wastes, formerly treasured alliances,
    Become proofs which can't be measured,
        Thrown and tossed, forever lost
            When consuming fragments of nature's whims
          Amass upon them.

            "A rest and all will be well…"
            Portends its death.

            This is not fatalism.

Reality awakens with the dawn,
    Restraining momentum from yesterday's beginnings.
        Drawn and drugged, victims seek passage.
            Freedom reigns for hardier boys and grown-up
girls.

Swelling tidal pools swirl against time until surrender is won.
    Against these forces who can stand?
        Resistance rewards the faithful without promise or
    compromise
          When waves, unceasing, return, breaking upon
        shores,
            Reveling in forces they alone contrive.

  Agendas are not hidden; rather, revealed within the serum's
               foam.

          The weak inherit nothing.
       The meek, though spurned, gain pelf,
        The stronger, surer, flourish.
        And life rewards itself.

Truth's undying siren's calls float above coursing tumults,
reassuring any who perceive,
    To stop, hear, and listening, cleave.
      Learn.
         Abide and reproduce.
           Your loins crave sons and daughters.

Patience is not virtuous; it is required.
    Vitalized, patients' perspectives
        Reach beyond superficial expectations.
         Their rewards are sure.
           Compositions are of birth parentage and lasting
           lineage.

        Coming renewal is your next opportunity.

Decision

It comes as no surprise how difficult the good ones are to make
and uphold.
>Pain and pleasure reside together.
>Longings and losses live intertwined.

>>A curse and grace
>>Compete for place.
>>A sanctioned race
>>Shall one erase.

Solicitous postures invite those who enjoy righteousness to
participate
>While determination, not detriment, speaks to intent,
>context, and nobler contents of the heart.
>Contentment and laughter, arising from pure joy, fashion
>healing balms.
>Rising on new wings, celebrations are born!

Visits and vistas voice varied opinions, dwelling in creatively
stimulating opportunities, where, as one leans one way, the
other, that.
>Sweet sips from fruits of sequestered fields lift souls and
>revive the weary, soothing aches of war-torn hearts
>With sweeping motions that invigorate the senses.
>Renewed, lingering passions caress joys in fresh
>expressions.

Life, in a moment, is passed from one to another.
>Within two hearts, minds and emotions combine.
>Conversations and feelings ebb and flow.
>Engaged, the newcomer is awestruck at a degree of
>authenticity heretofore unknown.

If this is a charade, should not all partake in its drama?
    A script for the first frames the story for the next.
    One wonders at a wanderer who dares venture into
    these pleasures,
    Knowing not what she will encounter.

According to the dictates of a heart's rationale,
    Mutual friendships seek balanced truth.
    Theirs are experiences enjoyed and savored,
    As one who is older, rekindles an ember.

        Precious are times,
        In recurring seasons,
    Whose choices bear good fruit
        Regardless of reasons.

Supporting the best and even the better,
    They go forth and are found faithful
    For living, forgiving, and for fulfilling.
    They are immeasurably happy.

Crowds, fresh on this scene, admire, enjoy, envy, and criticize.
    They, too, may bask in unwrapping these presents
    Should they wander down similar paths.
    Perhaps they will.

    Enjoy the dances of the featured ones.
    Remember your turn is coming.

Degrees

Commentaries, entrenched in attitudes, unclothe a struggling
actor,
> Whose prayers have gone Unanswered.
> Small and trivial, activities reveal work, walk, and will.
>> What objects, these?
>> Who demurs?

> Nature exposes intent.
> We stand amazed that the rites of truth
>> Have bent the bow
>> But not to breaking.

Aimless wandering rests in personal and inward potency.
> This is where pathos and passion remain.
> Invigoratedandrelativelyuntouched,tenacityisunmoved
>> Though through generations of strife
>> It has striven to survive.

Marvel at this recurrence.

Depths

The goose and the gander though fenced in together,
   Slander the crowds who have come to see whether
What's good for the goose are the goods for the gander
For trappings of both are the plagues of their grandeur.

Crevasses traverse unending hills, compelling rivulets collect;
   Descending precipices, stony heights, forbidden,
   isolated,
   They mock gravity and the grave.
   Bid them no heed, will you?

Grooves, pitiful, wherein life is smothered, are stifled and
choked,
   Burned, robbed of breath, and stricken with grief.
   Scorched beyond healing,
   They call your name.

Awaked from covered pyres they may still arise as does Spring
foliage.
   Thy pain is purification, a passage,
   Or so it is declared.
   Where is your resolve?

Depths linger, altered treasures' troves galore glare at the
unsuspecting.
   Washed glory adorns emerging flows;
   Crown the tall peaks!
   Energy and love unite.

Fissures mark paths in a mountain's story.
>Collected trailers, forged of flowing lava, form molten
>rivers.
>These descend toward moisture-laden, undulating pools.
>Immersed and breaking free, streaming steams' wispy
>clouds ascend.

Bid them well!
>Deserving feet yearn for fresh heights and cleansed air.
>Fulfilled minds and inquisitive souls long to dwell
>In scenes of Playful Abundance.

Not a promise,
>Nor a premise,
>Yet, laughing at fatalism:
>These are guaranteed to be good.

Emboldened but insignificant, a universe of gall,
>Genuinely ingenuous,
>Lies, shattered.
>May it rest in pieces, to the four winds, scattered.

It shall not reassemble itself.

Distribution

Brushed with greatness,
    A leaf turns in its concluding chapter.
    It lingers in an unmarked pile
    Blown, composing shapeless patterns,
    Blanketing surroundings as folds of carpeting are woven
    at will.

        Deference paid is confidence laid,
        Molded to the making of a man.

Entwined grasps, tighter hugs that will not release, yet,
    The touch of the common and the uncommon,
    Seen through opaque windows and caressed with tender
    hands,
    Whose mirth, while melodies brighten the room,
    Offer seasoned greetings with gestures of peace.

Health, a pleasing certitude, declarative of truth, recognized
        forever, comes.

Submission resonates.
    She expurgates torn up cloths, childish ornaments, and
    broken relics.
    Values remain.
    Will this one face coming eons apart from menace?
    She must be ready.

        What is known becomes the real.
        What is real retains appeal.

Relish mementos.
    Embellish life.
    Lift the ordinary.
    Broaden horizon's scenes.
    Turn another leaf.

Do

A silent walk,
A longer "I'll,"
The white-eyed forms
Adhere to style.

       Quivering,
       This bow is taut.
       Though bent and strained,
       It teaches naught.

Without hesitancy, reserved,
  A life's times' changes rebound then recoil
  Until head, hands, and hearts
  Realize the admeasurements of their cooperative
bargains.

   They cannot be separated in any way.

Covenant-bound, youthful alignments test adult resolve.
  They always do.
  Rifts, as they come, may be bridged in agreements
  From which doubt flees, as light dissuades
  darkness.

Foretell it; you speak truth.
  Eyes do; ears, too.
  These will not perceive or receive apart from intensely
  personal experiences.
  Togetherness only proffers more than imagination.

A weirdness of wealth
  In sickness or health,
  Measures nothing in time
  By waving scrawny hands and conjuring potions.

Echo

Small emissions evoke keen interest.
    Boomeranged, they remind masters of their unique
    origins.
    Hovering, morning mists shroud this party's merry and
    lilting tunes
    While dancers flitter and flutter for they are friendly co-
    habitants.

Somehow, explorations and contemplations cooperate,
    Nurturing each the other
    Beyond artificial borders.
    These, collected, invite renewed health and bid
    harmonies increase.

A pleasant stroll in cleaner air refreshes the mind and the body's
soul.
    Void of obstructions, freedom is not prevented.
    Past duty's pasty recollections
    Are placed in their respective boxes without undue
    negativity.

Fresh rays arouse long-neglected senses.
    Warmed and adaptable, flowing and serene,
    Comfort lingers as pleasures multiply.
    Peace-filled journeys attend those who venture forth.

Playful, they wander over unfamiliar paths,
    Discovering lights,
    Unrestricted sights,
    Evidence of ancient obsessions.

Earthen mounds,
    Temporary but long-tested,
    Rehearse endurance
    Against distant sounds and waves of toil.

Only time stands between what was and what is.
    Viewing from afar wonderers gaze intently at those who
    rise and fall,
    Contemplating, learning, leaning, living, admiring,
    Abiding, secure.

Hooks and clasps,
    Strings and ropes, severed,
    Allow former captives to possess larger lands,
    Bounded, but not with impenetrable fences.

Within these opportunities revived and revitalized souls test
their resolve,
    And, perhaps, run.
    Pushing homeward, they strain toward their finish.
    Crossing immense thresholds, they welcome their rest.

Warm embraces await them.
    Secure lodgings beckon those who risk.
    Embark on The Return.
    Victors, on arrival, are here to stay.

Effortless

Intervening, a softening caress, awash in solitude,
   A solo,
      A soaring obbligato, alone yet connected,
         Lifts essence while chorused voices capitulate,
           Supporting transcendence.

    It is sheer and unfettered harmony-infused sublimity.
           Receive its warmth.

Indolence's interruptions enjoy little meaning and are barely
noticed here.
     Should they demean a gift with disgust
       They simply dissolve into withering dust.
         Sadly, they belong to familiar experiences.
          They shall not be given credence again.

        Longed-for places, times, and seasons,
       Bathed in quests for love's pure reasons,
          Relish rhyming melodies
         And rise above cacophonies.

Who battles over obtuse agendas and meaningless controversy?
    At great costs to themselves and those for whom they say
they care,
      Their points have to be made.
        Loss is a deserted place, a vacuum.
         Songs of truth cannot resonate there.

A container of continuum indwells the searcher's being.
    May it satiate ravenous hunger?
      Fill it to overflowing.
        Organic balance will return.
         It will never need replenishing.

A peace desired,
   A piece acquired,
      Is discovered
         Or manufactured
            By those who dwell in quiet homes
               Where lofty expressions
                  Search for longing hearts,
                     Readied fingers, and
                        Tuned instruments.

Embrace

Responses and responsibilities evade the unwilling.

Silence implodes on itself.
    Metallic and unfeeling,
        Barbed hammers pound unceasingly on worn-out,
      lackluster strings.
          Soon these break.
            Stifled and arrested expressions are smothered,
              Quenching loves that wile the unsuspecting.

Crossings cease because they are forbidden.

Contemporary and hastily built structures teeter.
    They fall and float away on destructive undercurrents.
    Emitted and flung madly about,
        Insidious forces, coughed up from the bowels,
      Flow unchecked.

Dam the stream.

Commands refused, longings spurned,
    Lessons absent an instructor, a room, and class, fall on no
    ears.
        Distant and distraught distractions
          Compel the I.Q. toward abandon,
            Meant only as efforts to thwart braver conquests,
          Never winning prizes only imagined.

You cannot depart this quest although its success hangs as a
tear drop on a twig.

Reprimanded, ones without visions,
  Perceivedthroughexposedinsecuritiesandmelancholicwhining,
    Illuminate an abundance of extremes.
        Racing accusations
          Stifle the air,
              Voraciously mangling fruits,
                  Turning a once bounteous harvest
                    Into blackened destruction.

      This is the wake of its awakening!

Shaken in unbelief, ingratitude swells,
    Bold in its convergence
        With departures of freedom's license and liberty.
          Instantly instigated, regressing then flowing,
            Repeating themes,
              Repeating themes,
                The growing forms
                    Of singular isolationism's discomforts
                      Brazenly occupy
                        Broken places.

      They must fulfill their duty ere they fade.

Exit the fouled encounter.
    Admit, for to submit is to yield to forced insolvency where
    most dwell.
        This is stupidity.
          Released,
              Prevailing energies remember and move on.
                Caught and captured, then cultivated,
                  Thriving takes its rightful place—
                      Enraptured in a blessed embrace.

      Dreaming, it arouses itself once more.

Enrichment

Circled girders sustain parallels, decrying weaker structures.
    Ancients erected this.
        Laborers by the thousands contributed crafts.
        Magnificence reigned and endures.
        Witness's eyes, mystified, marvel at   returning
        stares.

Hunger pangs subside when holistic nutrients nourish and
energize the being.
    Mystics experience this.
        Salves, balms, and oils bathe dried skins and
        parched lips.
        Feeling the souls, fresh-caught idylls adorn
        ancient settees.
        Warmthsurroundsresiduesofcoldabandonment.

Times and tempests dissolve within history's cascades.
    Eternity exceeds this.
        Sparkling eddies loosen unruly knots.
        These ease their grips and dissolve their clots.
        Former and formidable foes become friends.

Rested, clasping fingers, assured in their reaches, open in
reverential awe.
    A memory ensures this.
        Swelling music pervades the hall and adjacent
        rooms.
        Surrounded by permutations, beacons of love's
        laughter
        Learn their ways toward life!

    Return O Beautiful One. Shine in your freedom's ring.

Stripped but alive, hordes, left to rot in smelly quagmires, thrice
are ostracized.
    They won't endure this.
        These respond to grace in reverential awe.
        Interlaced, woven, lightly fingered, and dainty
        mesh soften the brutish.
        The remaking is remarkable.

Remonstration's resolutions resound.
    Learners expect this.
        Undulations heed solicitous calls for silence or
        solitude.
        Cleansed, risk-takers deepen their breaths
        As they do their resolve.

Dispelling grievances, consumed, negativity's authors fail.
    Leaders embrace this.
        Natural entrances entrap and release energies
        from unknown sources.
        Giving all they possess, living ones reawaken their
        soulful experiences.
        The results are undeniable—these are
        emancipated.

        No longer tinged, shrouded, and mired,
          Meandering, savored mediocrities
          Yield to purpose, restoring the soul.
    These excel beyond expectations and wonder at their
          transformations.

Enter

Come aside.
    Pick your place.
        Kneel.
            Position respite and cease from labor.

Mingle thoughts freely with hope.
    Dream.
        Carry starry-eyed glances inward.
            Heaven's rewards await your rest.

Curtail all else.
    Acquired wings lift the most humble of creatures away.
        This adventure takes time.
            A gift of prescience welcomes the learner.

Meaning shapes memory.
    Strengthened resolutions mold revolutions.
        Renewal's essence freely flows
            Where opportunity emerges from contemplation's
        deep harmonies.

Conscious choices ponder wondering lusts.
    These savor tastes of soulful meditations,
        Leaving precise measurements of structured
        expectations
            Unarmed and unalarmed.

Entering a sweet intermission, ordinary demands are arrested.

        Go toward the Light with all your might.

Epic

                    I rate.

Injustice imprisons feeble, frail, fault-ridden, and foolish
parishioners.
Instinct pushes parental forces to enter the fray!
Usherspranceupontheirdandy'spraisedadmonitions—
only to drop their transmissions when next confronted
with life's even simplest challenges.
No longer optional, the nets are flung upon the unwilling
who flail and fall, suddenly realizing their entrapments.

Incredulity wonders at the bold manipulation and its greed.
Perspiration and inspiration precede true greatness but few
                    understand this.
The masses look for easiest ways to recount the reasons why
                    "It is not impossible."

Freed,silencedvoices,regenerated,callforthutterances
never heard,
Whispering to educated and eon-laden wiser ones,
"Come apart."
Peace replies, then returns rejuvenated.
Cautious at first, paces quicken as longings hasten
toward Eternal Light.

No things dark inhibit or inhabit enlightened faces.

Running wild, freedom sets its own pace while roaming
unfettered amid strong and threatening towers,
unmolested.

Intrusiveandinsolentspeech-makers,thoughconquered,
still emit ineptitude's accusatory utterances, flowing
incessantly, even as they descend into their personal
hells.
Their mystery's unknowns,
Thankfully,
Rule temporarily, though without remorse.
Mindfully unaware, they heed no coming demise.

Greater causes grant learned positions to those who deliberate
and liberate themselves.

They are the mindful and respected.
Few in the crowds of simpletons comprehend.
They don't want to.
Presented with emboldened receptors,
Enlightenment searches for an Enduring One.
Uncharted vistas reveal intoxicating interrogatories.
Despite pervasive though inconsequential and unnerving
interruptions, steadied and true-hearted pilgrims survive
and press on.
Opposing and shallow inconclusiveness will bow its
weary head, finally, when shown for what it really is.

Manicured images abound and dare to stand against those who
would turn and stand alone.

Committedstill,insurgentssomehow,inexorablyclaimunmerited
prizes, entrapping feeble souls.
Leaning and feeding on unpretentious servants,
They gloat and mock truer-hearted pilgrims
Or demand realignment and altered allegiance.
Shall not the good possess their inheritance free of
encumbering error?
Yes, in time—but in a long time.

The festooned phases of morose and meaningless encounters
and mockingly distasteful demonstrations from self-proclaimed
prophets and profiteers will be shown to be merely masquerades
and simple, silly charades, the actions from the play book a con
man manufactures, promotes, and parades.

Passages and Passengers transcend haplessly heaped,
vaguely cognitive, and contrived utterances, along with their
accompanied blissfully-intentioned obscurities.
Their originators know exactly what they are doing,
As do the captured who break free.

Exchange

Behind smiling eyes, smirking at notions of an easy heist,
deception lurks.
    Crafting lying propositions, gentle introductions confound
    the innocent and control the unsuspecting.
        An expected bounty forever lost pales in value to its
        cost,
            When what's returned surpasses greed
            And ever fails to fill the need.

Violated, foolish and forgetful ones confuse the familiar with the
neglected.
    Trying to untie the strands that bind them,
        They forge the chains that long confined them.
            Stories, retold countless times, fall upon deafened ears.
        Abandoned roads hold dark secrets.
            Blind men's fatal adventures happened here.

When the costs of the journey exceed the value of its souvenirs
    A large and wasteful void consumes the traveler.
        Already weary, the travailing soul faints.
        Wads of currency fail to satisfy debts.
        Shortchanged and doubting,
            One looks for assuring eyes
            And finds emptiness.

Betrothed and betrayed, unwittingly forlorn ones bemoan their
fates.
    Manufactured without comprehension, their wasted remains
    mold and rot.
        Ignorance is not bliss.
            Chagrined, losers cower at this.
            Others don't care at all.
               No matter, the unjust will get theirs
                But not from the ones who have suffered.
    Injustice is uncovered, uncomfortable, and unrequited.

Crimes of cruelty poison future relationships.
Travesty's legacies last a very long time.
While forgiven for release, a memory keeps its piece.
Stung and recoiling at sharp, unending pain,
Past accounts will not be reconciled
To anyone's satisfaction.
Former health may not return,
Sleeking stealthily away,
Dying slowly.

When will infusions of living energy and organically grown
harvests occur?
Pills to cure ills are merely drugs to numb acute sufferings of the
dependent.
Independence and peaceful coexistence require more.

Explanations

Seized in its season,
    Reason fails
        When silence engulfs a carefully designed roster of
        duties,
            Whence, flowering, neither glory is transcended,
            Nor a scene fulfilled.

No explanations are offered but with parsing, in time,
    Money and energy are sought and left in suspended
    animation.
        Myriads relate.
            Gone are their lights.
                Frightened by intense negativity,
                    Inequity, inequality, and iniquity prosper
                        Where weeds are permitted to bloom,
                        Choking hearty seeds.

Knowledge is not powerful
    When it fashions utter emptiness.
        Distraught, its owner wanders through unfelt and coarse
        apparitions,
            Indistinct, unmoved, and quiet.

Colder seasons follow on.
    One upon another they come,
        Festering, fomenting diseases
            As warmth and comforts fade
                Into expanding distances, irretrievable.

These are the bitter memories
Of what was not,
Regrettably sad
In all that never was.

Comprehension flees even as it is pursued.
Entrapped, the seeker, though in earnest view of what might
have been,
Shatters the looking glass.
In disillusioned and impassionate sorrow
He falls to his knees, faces the wall,
Crying rivers of tears,
Flowing dolefully.

Even these are sold to the highest bidders.
These people are scum.
Descending to unending and demoralizing depths,
Desperation nearly consumes, and consummates
destruction.

Return to the Gift
Or remain within the curse.

Factor

The immediate supersedes the important.
>   Verbiage devours trees, bloats libraries, and consumes
>   airways.
>   It contributes little to creativity's impetus.

Robotic assemblies replace humane interaction's warmth.
>   Hisses mixed with digital audio substitute the former
>   with the false.
>   A mockery of truth has taken hold and grips the senses.

Does it matter?

If reasons yearn for masks then let them be worn and hide gross
errors.
>   Is a covering only for a puritan's head?
>   No, if what is concealed needs to be.

Eagles fly freely and hunt the prey upon which their lives
depend.
>   Rhythm, like water, seeks its own level.
>   Death occurs when gross mistakes consume their
>   authors.

Truth desires more.
>   Let the silenced ones cleanse their minds, heal their
>   hearts,
>   Form fewer words, and fortify their will.

Stained garments endure beyond the tragic events with which
they were intimately acquainted.
>   The wearers were brushed aside and bruised.
>   These stand and are counted when their times come.

Turning and churning, rotating blades burn to understand and
to be understood.
Noiseless figurines alone shoulder no responsibility, and
they shouldn't.
They are rarely noticed.

Memories, dimmed through tedium, dwell in lost, though sacred,
insecurities
Until lightning's beams pierce the brokenness, declaring
with voices that obliterate the voids,
"You can live again if this is your desire."

Wait!
Consider the implications of this call.
You will be part of the conflict and the conquest, no
matter who wins.

Ineptly, though focused, possessing ingratiating attitudes,
unleashed foes spew forth gross intimidations.
They would distract the committed and discourage the
faithful if they could.
They will control plentiful numbers of those who err but
not in sufficient quantity to claim the ultimate triumph.

Changed patterns challenge partnerships and alter life.

Following what courses does fortitude reposition sources and
marshal its forces?
Coarse currents cleave to rocks they consume, remaking
their landscapes.
Lava flows compose wonders to onlookers and caution
for sojourners.

On the path of long endeavor
Weigh your degrees of participation carefully.
Once embarked, there is no return for ones with
determination.

Fallen

Rise, though crippled, braced once more for battle, and break
the patterns of defeat.
    The beastly claws of the enemy carved grotesque
impressions upon the earth.
      Mapped in legends of rhythmic paces,
        Their mighty swords and shields
          Defeated the desires
            Of those who were dashed
              Against the walls of their wills.

    The evil ones appeared to win the contest this time.

Quite suddenly, however, bold alternatives appeared.
    Horizons of hope from former days, though dimmed,
      Once bowing to feigned options and clairvoyant
      messages
        Even though proven unreliable,
          Were rejuvenated with the coming of the dawn.

    The balance was upset in favor of the blessed.

Revelers come for they have been invited.
    Tuned tones of truth pervade this new dwelling place for
    awhile.
      Colorful palettes, re-inserted into this composition,
        Contribute altered perspectives.
        There is joy in the camp.

Too soon sacrificed, then severed, a commander learns he's
dead.
    In his youth he had noticed a tiny fish in its small confine,
    suffering.
        He sought to rescue it but he could not.
          Timed and suspended breath cannot be held for too
        long.
            The slightest touch with best intent or ill
              Enlivens or exterminates a one with weakened
          will.

Casually, accidental contact permanently changed the courses,
    A profound surprise!
      What relief!
        Elimination never felt so good.
          The chaff of needless relations is disbursed.
          Grounds glisten with dew.

        Come, new seasons.

Survival had waned, was beaten, but restored.
    Unsearchable and virtually blinded to truth, the commander
    asks,
        "When doors slam shut and seal this doom, how may they
        be opened?"
          A small one whispers, "I possess the key!"
          "Use me."

Fist

Clasped, a fist in a palm, an owner's servile, sterile, and drawn
smiles mask truer motives.
   Small-talk evades inquisitive eyes and ears for only
   a short time.
   Contemporaneous speech-makers wither against
   unstable, crumbling walls.
   Removed to trash heaps with their bearers, their jobs are
   finished.
   Isolated, they become one with their devotees.

Longing's terseness
   Invades quietude's abodes,
      Places for those who hunger for endless exploration.
         Quilted words remain unheard,
            Isolated souls, unstirred,
               Marking lines and passing days.

Decry a restless spirit.
   In vain shall grow the crawling vine,
      Through long and lonesome valleys pine
         For golden riches to possess,
            But clutching does not find caress.
               Unless redeemed,
                  It languishes in cyclical desperation.

Scripts are played before they're read.
   A stage hands only markers to unwitting and foolish
   actors.
   Playbill commentaries "Thank you for your
   support."
   Periodic graces greet souls alone.
   Prompt and courteous nods wish: "All is well."

In step, friends say they understand.
    They don't.
        Expectations dashed, they die.
          Surrender meets a wandering eye.
            Resurrect a patient's woes.
              In deeper pain their story grows.
             Finery codifies its end.
                Greed controls the ones who lend.

Clenched no longer, you must release yourself from that which
you neither owned nor owed.

Force

Gruesome creatures bearing bizarre features inhabit the hole.
        Touch generates deep yearnings for the revealed
        "There must be more."
        Wholly tuned to perspiring and exhaustive recompense,
        Applications command, "Fill in the blanks."
        Conflicts pervade the good and goods inherit their evils.

Contentment flees as shallow ponds evaporate on stilled and
warming mornings.
        This struggle never ceases.
        Wrestle an opponent to the death for allegiances that
        last!
        Callused leaders can be removed.
        Unknown battles in a forced field bid brothers
        fight each other.

Nuisances not yet conspicuous
        Live in mirages of minds and means.
        Similarities tell us so.
        Fleeting and darting shadows learn to obey commands
        of Higher Directives.
        They must.

To not know reasoned explanations,
        Victims of intrusions anyway, and in disorderly ways,
        Follow blindly,
        Consumed by forces
        Before and beyond them.

Folly is the food of fools.
> Subservient to self-possessing hunger
> Slaves tend gardens of the takers, then fold and expire.
> Carving sufficient spaces for new generations
> The rusty implements continue to be used and
> contaminate the soil.

Life's rhythms undulate, uninhibited, 'mid sequestered futures,
but bolstered in hope.
> A history's "yes" bespeaks demise and rebirth, an
> unbending and eternal earth.
> Cowered, small endeavors yield and give their victims,
> cages.
> Courageous undertakings' weapons shall win their wars
> in stages.
> Ritual choices unmask countless and multi-dimensional
> destinies.

Foul

Dreaded outer fences, barbed-wire defenses of warped
realizations,
    Grab the unsuspecting,
      Control the tactics,
        Inflict deep and painful wounds,
         And fool the careless.

        A trap.
Over what desires for reduction does obliging reign?
      Now here or nowhere?

Inserted, mercenary ones punch through, forcing frenzied
feedings,
    Berating their foes,
      Gorging their beings without regard to the effects of
gluttony.
        Some die.

  Chanted recitatives deny speculation and prevent creative
        thought.

Control, cowering, raises conflicts and contradictions.
    Stab the heart of this beast.
      Destroy its death-blows.

Self-promulgated, masses and messes expand and contract,
    Lustfully inhaling resources.
      Dull, confused, and abused,
        These locust-invasions consume nearly all they
        touch.

They fall, however, of their own weight.
  Unseeing their contentious courses' outcomes,
    They fumble and stumble in plain view of all.

It was bound to come.
  Tricked by their own craftiness,
    They lie confused, conquered, quiet, and dead.

                Simple resistance did it.

Crassness is cremated.
  Its ashes dissolve into oblivion.
    The useless obligations are no more.

Peaceful inhabitants, jealous of fortitude and, in silent resolve,
  Rightfully place sacrilege's dissipation before stronger
  winds.
    These are the proofs of the natures of their being.

Bitter tongues are consumed, suffocating on dreadful and
malicious words.
  Purity's convalescence lets its soul breathe again.
    The chains are gone, the boundaries removed, once and
    for all.

Gentle

Phrases bespeak their origins' styles of delivery
    Where intent is revealed,
        Disguises are removed,
           Love is borne, and
               Beautiful smiles grace countenances.

                In a soft kiss
      Dwell a tenderness of heart and a kindness of tongue.

Scenes, worthy of remembrance, return;
      Hope's fortunes may yet come to pass where love's
      visitations will.

Too close is not too far,
    Too much is not enough.
        Two longings' fare is sure.
           Drawn-closer love is tough.

Secure in what has never been, the past recites lofty tales of
what is to come.
    Where one desires growth to bear
        A fruit within its season,
           So marks the pattern of the times
              In step with rhymes and reason.

Eyes lift and gracious, loving hands touch outer realms' inward
soul.
    Words of reckoning
        In familiar phrases
            Remake teachable hearts
              Toward a fondness of the fair.

At peace, hands unfolded, caress.

Greatest Song Among Men

Let us listen to the song of Christmas again.
Now once more we'll hear the story of God among men,
      The birth of our Lord,
      The baby adored
      By angels of number untold,
      The humble stable,
      The star up above,
      And the story never grows old.

Mary, Joseph, and the inn without a space,
God's great care and love provided another place:
      The grandest announcement
      To shepherds, amazed,
      That shattered the night so still,
      That peace had come down from Heaven to Earth
      So that all might live in good will.

And three wise men who brought gifts of precious worth
Bowed so low to worship the King Who came down to Earth.
      Christ Jesus, so humble
      Was born here below
      To ransom all souls from sin.
      O the wonder of that first Christmas night
      Is the greatest song among men.

Hear

Impulse cares little for simple, ordinary tasks.
 Cycle's conveniences stymie more important projects
   without lenience.

Conversation ceases when absence is demanded.
 Solo instrumentals fade from loftier themes, disbanded.

   Drawn back folds of an old, tattered scrim,
    Call out intentions to her, then to him:
     Craft yet another interpretive hymn
    To alter your sequence, unbowed to a whim.

Quests for patterned partnering wane,
 Their efforts declining
   When coarse impositions
    Invade and reside.

Above sweltering hemispheres lovely echoes are not heard.
 Rather, they wander,
   Circling,
    Searching for homes.

     Knowledge?
    Little is recalled.
     Feelings?
   These bear few residual memories.

Those of ten thousand are sorted, sifted, discarded, or
   treasured.

Closing the matter fails to come quickly enough.
    Its lateness testifies to the indolence of its misguided
    directors,
        Lenders, whose feigned shock and surprise at their own
        insufficiencies,
            Fool no one.
                Hardly do these malcontents
                  Consider their effects.
                    They care not at all.

                Nomenclature garbles intent.
       These are the times when words are useless.

Softer and interconnected exchanges dwell in tender
submission,
    Sublime movements in weaving patterns of sensitivity and
    love,
        Quelling tedious and useless utterances.

Equanimity replaces claustrophobic environs.
    Inhabitants are freed of the chains forged by those
        Whose causes under guises of compassion and reaching
            Are nothing more than control and domination.

Forging heretofore unknown paths, enlivened seekers
    Squelch the critical,
        Quench the spiritualists, and
            Promote creative geniuses of inspired inquirers.

Inheritance lives beyond mere existence,
    Awaiting those released from superficial dealings.
        Coming in stillness, essence awakens as thunder rolls.
        It shall not be denied to eager ones
            Who seek it earnestly enough.

Horizon

The fire is out.

Consumed and neglected ashes wait to be removed, or simply
blow away.
   Distant mountains' lengthening shadows recall past
engagements.
      Energies subside as sunset comes.
         When, quite suddenly, a mighty conqueror appears!
         No one withstands his unleashed furry.
            All are consumed, again.

Vainly clinging to hope, perched on steep and foreboding clefts,
   Tiny creatures, barely aware of their own existence,
      Attached to singularly secure outcroppings
         Known only to them,
            Are swept away, devoured, and
            crushed.

This power is beyond imagination.
   Its presence threatens most those who fear it least.
      Escape is forbidden.
         Unbridled endurance fights but wins the contest
         rarely.

Protect thine own
   As from sheltered environs
      You offer counsel
         Regarding other's fates!

A tie that binds fools feeble minds,
    Though signs warn of impending danger.
        Receptive ones, however, may respond.
            Though sounded alarms echo o'er the countryside
                Few heed these desperate prophecies.

Others seek solace
    Convergent populations provide.
        But these, too, are washed away
            With oncoming and violent storms.

From what sources does surety come?
    Who measures its strength and longevity?
        Old lessons teach younger learners that experience
    supersedes them.
            Dainty tracks, erased through time,
                Ne'er again tell tradition's tales.

All of worth passes this way eventually.
    Survival is not assured.
        Help, from within and without, calls to futures.
            Observers bow and eager ones learn from
            The Passing.

A struggle ensues.
    Conflicted voices shout for attention,
        Their remonstrations falling on deafened ears.
            Who should rely on formerly trusted alliances?
            Whom will you trust?

Collected relationships,
    Thriving, though not in triumph,
        Possess longevity and legacy
            In ones whose interests reach beyond the moment.

These few shape diverse destinies of many
    Whether or not attention is paid to them or they are
presented adulation.
        Those who endure fashion beginnings for unsuspecting,
blind trusts.
            Renewal takes varied forms.

Hours

Consonant rhythms inform the body of the time.
    We strain to not believe.
    Location subsists in locomotion.

Timed rest transcends sleep in stages of sustained anticipation.
    The felt need for more presses hard upon the travelers.
    No one understands until the baggage from their backs
    is lifted.

Unrestrained, walk, or run.

"While you were out
    Your world forever changed."
    Or did you?

Contributions to the contrary, a political acceptance was
greedily bought.
    Stirring conflict in the core, its authors cared little.
    "It appears we have abandoned our original directives."

Events, issues at odds until resolved, foment impending
revolutions.
    In-tuned wholeness was cast aside for more convenient
    methods
    When allowed and greeted warmly by ones who travel
    extensively.

Sojourn is travail when moved beyond the pale.

Covet what you know is yours.
      Covenant with those whose associations bring life.
      Horde the hours and earn the powers.
      Use them well lest they abuse their own.

Safe journey.

Image

To pacify the pains they feel
The image makers mask the real.
Flaunting beauty, bathed in light,
Their souls beneath are veiled from sight.

The ones whose lives would shun disease
Present facades designed to tease.
To blinded eyes, no faults reveal
What image maker's thoughts conceal,
While hiding elements of shame
Remains the goal within this game.

Crude observations from the crowd
Contrast the wonderfully endowed.
Their jealous streaks and long applause
Portray the natures of their cause:
Possess a form that few reflect,
And falling short, to feign respect.

Injustice pounds its fist-demand
On futile hopes imagined, planned
To rest on shoreline's distant views,
When bullish, lying men confuse
Heart's true desires, never won,
And mourning passers leave, undone.

Not so the ones whose image-forms
Compose the calm and conquer storms.
Intense, their inward struggle strains
To forge the strengths, to rend the chains
Which bind the captives without cause,
To free the slaves from death grip's jaws.

Festooned charades parade and pair
The ones who openly declare
They're born and destined to perform
A metamorphosis, a norm.

Through tiny fissures, bends, and cracks,
The Steady Forces launch attacks
To tear the body of the beast,
Restraining none 'til war is ceased.

The Story, arduous to tell,
Emboldened, Means become its Hell.
With crowd's approvals stored, embraced
Beneath the surface, they're disgraced.

To leave despairingly, to run,
Or stay and fight as all for one?
Consideration's wiser choice
Gives rapt attention to a voice
Who beckons, "Live the life you've got
Instead of dying while you rot."

The fundamentals shriek and gape
While they're the ones whose swift escape
From gross conditions, if they could
Would render value toward their good.
Destroy the dungeons of the fake.
The freed will live for living's sake.

Imbued

Attend an altered image, crafted from out, not in.
    It spins in awe and wonders at wellness.

        Open arms and empty hands
      Sift shifting sands without demands.

Orbed delights crave glimpses of sight,
    As lightning and thunder cascade upon the mountains,
    Dissolving to strange and welcomed calms:
    Balms in innermost regions,
    Not imbued with artifacts' contrivances.

Pulsed and primal, impaled through imprisonment,
    A pauper is a poured-out cup,
    Valued in pretense alone.

Bereft of want and excess,
    There is no one
    To lead the weary through safe passage,
    To discover gifts that never were.

        Nothing bores a righted wrong.
      Fault and shadow wring the throng.

Tokens of dismissed amity,
    Graceless gestures, tepid smiles,
    Darkened eyes of the spurned and destitute
    Pervade the simple and confound the wise.

Inertia

The cache is not full.
>Rooms for relinquishing and replenishing occupy the same structure.
>Imposition, an imposter, begs for status and, remarkably, its wish is granted.
>Read through tiny spectacles, distorted images reveal no assurances.
>Broken promises infuse alliances, inflamed on fleeting fantasies.

Where is acceptance?
>Reveling in oddity, pleasures form and reform the necessities of being.
>Introspection subs its place.
>Languishing in ineptitude, dependent ones crawl toward primal cravings.
>They are lost.

Allotments, given grudgingly, spare their truth, casting fragments to the hungry.
>A tempo, tempests swell in returning onslaughts,
>Waving greetings and departures
>As destruction precedes and follows its prey.
>There is no escape.

Do fevered pitches favor an open hand or recoil from slaps and twists of the wrist?
>Fervor replaces none of what is truly sought.
>Settling is not requested; rather, bought.

Statistics poignantly prove their conclusions.
    Eras of haggling, hassle, and hand-me-downs proffer
improvised fittings.
    These are uncomfortable and disheveled.
    Eventually torn, they are dumped.
    Discarded and forgotten, no one remembers they ever
were.

Ill-informed and function-laden,
    The hapless shove each other through dark-webbed
entrapments,
    Fearing much,
    Conquering nothing,
    Immobilized nearly beyond recognition.

Spiraling down an endless shaft,
    Lengthened or shortened only by one's imagination,
    Their falls descend toward demoralization.
    For those who give up, these are the failures of sins.
    For those who want more, these are where living begins.

A clock turned round,
    An endless sound,
      A creaking floor,
        An empty store,

Forced rhythmic drops
    And dried-up mops,
      A broken vase,
        A worn-out case,

A dislodged nest,
    A weak behest,
      A cradled sigh,
        A blinded eye,

Dishonored laws,
Emboldened flaws,
A deafened ear,
A drifting tear,

Misguided grace,
A war torn place:
A tiny groan,
An unpaid loan.

The spindly, stiffened necks shall break
Upon the views opponents take.

Institution

The bottom of the barrel rests on the top of the mind.

A person fulfilled
Is the one most instilled
With the pains of the hearts
Who are dying.

The cries of the desperate
Sustained without respite
Are par for the throngs
Who cease trying.

Wishes not granted assured in the forums where stifling
restrictions abound,
Will falter and sputter in unsettled moments when burdensome
facts are unwound.

Purposed, stilled craving
For lives worth the saving,
Their actors
Provision the crowd.

Astounding the truth
Is that one from his youth
Could live for so long
In a shroud.

Tiered revelations belong to a servant who, in his cocoon,
dreams for more.
Proclaiming his story,
One moment of glory,
A flaw is revealed in the mix—

Though small won
It's not one
To notice
When just one
Comes onto the scene
With a fix.

Exposed as it's posed,
A photo of truth may still be re-touched.

Indigenous people,
Who bow to a steeple
Foretell the dissention
To come.

The times won't forget this,
So figure and set:
This is sure
As a formula's sum.

The rulers and gamers,
Once time-honored framers,
Whose hardened hearts
Cringe at their fall

Will seek satisfaction,
Though wanting of action
For no one
Will care to recall.

For only in minds
Of the souls are the kinds
Of relationships
Once long desired.

More oft are these tenured ones
Only remembered
As wonders
Not fully acquired.

Were nothing begun
From the life of just one
Where longings
And grasps were required,

The fruits of endeavor
Would cease altogether
And stillness
Would swallow the tired.

Invitation

Savor inward acceptance in orbiting, spiritual cravings, warming
to mounting desires.
>> Obey the gestures that wave you in.
>> Enjoy the full experiences that call your name.

Reason fashions its handiwork.
>> Hearts and hands portray their demands.
>> These beckon you.

Relax and wait.
>> Contemplate.
>> Then, create.

Burdens are lifted from those who yearn for gentle respite.
>> Tenderness, in quiet company, turns aside,
>> Soaring as souls decide.

Confusion diminishes a chorus, cursing inspiration, diverting
gazes to non-essentials.
>> The story's chapters compose a tallied toll on wearied
>> souls
>> Who simply wanted more.

Composure dreams of different scenes.
>> Resignation dwarfs but will not relinquish unaccompanied
>> longings.
>> They remain because they must.

Stillness, itself hidden, calls to ones who mock the race,
>> Requesting them to slow their pace,
>> Or stop it all together.

A reckoning, removed as naught is banned,
  Clasps a strong and stern demand,
  Stooping when the promised comes.

A banquet was prepared by hosts who mostly cared,
  Their joys of giving shared with foreigners
  Who never heard the song of "yes."

Stolen treasures
  Might be discovered
  But not by the ones who first searched.

While conversations move toward rapid conclusions,
  A learning of lures lives on
  While obligated and soiled ones toil without ceasing.

Guided connections take possession of tasks,
  Offering replacements and completing them well.
  These are better than origin's best.

Wave them on.

Islands

Slivers of hope live within those who endure sordid conflicts
as over newly discovered lands they tread softly, trying nearly
without breath, but mightily believing, that this can be done.
    Open spaces await diligent and hearty souls.
    Pursue—for many point the ways.

The circus clowns in hand-me-downs, set in former times, on
minor planes, burst with pride at multitudes who stare at the odd
and grotesque images they conger up.
    Aligning graceful limbs to passing whims,
        Their spirits bruised,
            They give out clues
                But few are smart enough to recognize them,
                  Or even listen.
    They are side shows.
    Treats can be sweet though offered from maligning
individuals.

Stifle or shuffle the dreams of those who've attempted to break
the bars of cages they've permitted their guards to construct.
    Isolated, as though trapped by the unknown, their
    sufferings are intensified, memorable, and terrible almost
    beyond words.
    Partaking misshapen portions from losers who chose
    their fates is the folly of followers whose wasted lives live
    only in records of the fallen, downtrodden, and cast out.

Brief retorts punctuating grueling rounds of questions will
probably not suffice the focused interrogator who would rather
ban the persons than attempt to access truth.
Pour over the testimonies of the captured.
Moreover, dwell on what their words don't say.
Cull the secrets from hidden ideas that if freely
expressed
Could change their worlds.
Scan the horizons for distant, enchanting lands.
How vast are the urges that beckon one home!

Alignments and confinements shall not satiate those who,
despite their chains, shall within a moment of protracted
strength, strain at vile bonds until they have torn and severed
them.
On behalf of these who languish alone, bid them
expressions of grace, strength, and endurance.
Better than that, help them.

Left

None are retained.
>Cooperation asks for engagement without exception.
>Requirements compel participation, unwilling or free.
>Standing, observing from afar—these are no longer mere
>considerations.
>>You will come.
>>I will come.

There are no vacancies in the rooms of this abode.
>Corners are consumed with the presence of uninvited
>visitors.
>Niches, filled as tumblers to overflowing, have been
>scrubbed to eradicate dead cells.
>These voids are occupied with living organisms.
>>Waves of emotion speak eternal change.
>>None can stop or constrain them.

Benchmarks erode with timed passages and unwavering
pressures.
>Extraneous sources mark their presence indelibly.
>Rhythms fancy themselves whole unto themselves.
>They leave few traces.
>>In dim repositories
>>Resides the temporal.

Lines

Uttered, drawn, abandoned, dropped,
Painted, squared, curved, and marked,
Dotted, bold, drooped, and broken,
Crossing, wavy, thick, and thin

They invade.
    They're everywhere.
        They pervade, permeate, skewing vision, or enhancing it.
      No matter:
          Convergence comes through infinity's canvasses
         In between the lines
           Or in spite of them.

Fragile, fallen, strengthened, still,
Remaining, coursing, intersecting,
They close upon
The Captives.

Opened awareness,
   Reigning free,
     Is now confined.
       Destined ones glimpse,
        Observing their past,
       Break free,
         And cry out.

Cherished are the words of the imprisoned.
Hear them and hearken to their messages.
They reflect intentionally composed elements
Whose futures are doomed to erasure apart from rescue.

When thoughts are bound,
    Divorced from fresh perspectives,
        Timidity sleeks,
            Cowering behind immense, barbed, chain-linked
            fences
                Where futures
                    Can be seen
                        But not won.

With unbridled force
Captors control the impoverished,
Preventing them from reigning or running wild
In living quests for meaning and motive.

For those fortunate enough
    Not to be victims of marauding conquests,
        Lines to receive and don weapons
            Are not long.
                (Should they repose
                    Their species shall bow
                        To winds of forced domination.)

Align with mightier friends,
Who, even though unseen,
Surely have armed the outer defenses,
Preparing for constant war.

Discern their power,
    Learn their knowledge.
        Apply their wisdom.
            These compose stronger lines,
                Words, groupings,
                    Networks,
                        Giving life.

Links

Strong ties, wrapped as strands of three or more, are virtually
impossible to rend.
> Shall we listen to chords of Higher Will?
> Unseen but protean, a collection of cords refuses the
> abodes of decaying residue.
> Loosen yourself from the shackles of insecurity.

> Grasp and clench steadfastly to properties spiritually
> borne
> Whose sources revealed,
> Bring liberty and privilege, contentment, and peace.

Within which shall you dwell,
> The farce, the frame, or farm?

Observe disparate scenes in this three-act drama.
> Design your own exit.

Match

To light a flame,
     Compose a name,
     Become the same, a picture's frame,
And burn anew;

To turn the clock and start the round,
     To move as one in silence, found
     Feet planted firmly in fresh ground,
Who've played the game;

To raise the steeple and the spire,
     Become the symbols of desire
     Within their quests to truth, aspire,
These loaned their souls.

Bequeathed a legacy in form
     To other folks outside the norm
     Who fashioned naught against the storm
Through which they'll pass;

The endless wands of future's time
     Will push the limits from sublime
     To fashion movements not in rhyme
To ward increase;

But for the ones who run in place
     A wooden hurdle in that space
     Becomes a hindrance to the race
And taunts their minds.

Know peace within
    When struggles' win,
       Assured of conquest over sin,
As from the past to futures when

It shall remain.

Meal

Utilitarian wills fashion sealed enclosures.
    Wound, prison's barbed outer fencing deeply wounds
  seekers of expanding horizons.
      Thirsts and pangs for simple nourishments
        Cause craving's bearers to construct openings
       Through formidable barricades beyond
     perimeters,
        No matter pain, cost, or loss.

Rhythmic pulsations, beating,
    Regardless of their eon, by cosmic law,
      In force, meant for wrong doing,
        Shall not silence people of unwilling postures
      Who resist onslaughts
        Of those with temporal powers.

Individuals, destined to win or unwilling to lose—they're all
        included.

Seen by vast audiences,
    The "Aye's" are rearranged.
      Bearing few encouragements,
        They merge with those whose parched lips
       Could be satisfied
        With even the slightest moistures of truth.

Flows, restrained, seek common levels, basic understandings.
    These comprise a wilting group
      Whose dreams flower in motionless pictures,
        Composed of enhanced reflections,
        Whose possession of brushes and palettes
     Is a farce: a void.

For those who turn prematurely away,
    Shunning embraces of false solicitude,
        Personal discovery wills these momentary expressions
            Not to last.
                In which does life brood, birth, and bathe its
                newborns?
                    These are borne on brush strokes of the
                    eternal.

Latent and, too often, late,
    The child learns less then loses all.
        Trivialize historic legions and their lessons
            Whose legacies appear
                To be forever forgotten,
                And you lose.

                    Revive the Quests.
                    Revisit Stimulation.
            Refuse tradition's dying, lifeless forms.
            Revolt from staid and ordinary utterances.
                    Break free.

Feast on delectable dishes you've never tasted before.
    Set a table with fresh cloths and cutlery.
        You, and your guests who pay the fare,
            Enter and find your places.
                Those at this meal will dine,
                    Enjoying rich delicacies and delicious wine.

Mechanism

Strained cooperation twists and squirms, turning uninvited guests toward patronage.
> Unseeing, it tolerates and promotes vain hopes, futile dreams.
> Utilitarianism, behind grossly inflated language, fuels robotic tongues.
> They speak nothings to deafened ears and closeted minds.
> Emptied expressions are permutations unto themselves.
> Eyes avoid attestation as paper, plastic, and people flow.

Segmented, separated, isolated, they're mute as if sworn to secrecy.
> These beings move only as permitted.
> Day's lights yield to unending clocks, cloaking servitude in drudgery.
> Excessiveness fills too small a space.
> Silence ignores a cunning yet ineffectual welcome.
> Eagerness bids the passing adventurer to stop, turn, swear, and leave.

Immortalized ignorance purposes brief familiarity should recognition come.
> Picture broken stems.
> They cling by mere threads to tiny recollections.
> Load and lift their sorry glances.
> Shallow eyes bear sad romances.
> Capture reflections of whispered, open, and seething rebellion.

Faded perspectives haunt the houses of former times.
    Gentler and happier touches pervaded their scenes.
    These are no more.
    They were replaced by poorly crafted substitutions.
    Craving life, protagonists sought willing audiences to
    share the misery.
    They unearthed numerous interested patrons.

Lists force submission.
    Diminishing numbers yearn to unwind.
    Relaxation is unknown.
    Rest comes not to worn bodies,
    Excessively tried,
    Tired of trying.

Pause no more.
    Renew efforts.
    Produce unlikely consequences.
    Planned positions disclose outworn contrition,
    And suddenly are stale.
    Breaths long for the bar and stump the bored.

It is time.
    Yellowed carnivorous doors expand, welcoming
    mechanized, robotic souls.
    Inexplicably drawn,
    These trod feeble ways toward oblivion.
    Calamitous though it may be,
    Its rise and fall affects them all.

Memory

A life touches many lives.
    One of them was mine.
        Adventurous, numerous journeys into unknowns were
commonplace.
           The speed, the rush, the thrill, the chill,
                Formed waves of confidence, formerly still.

Laughter, with its contagious smile, was true,
    A heart-felt expression of closeness, friendship, and family.
        Lengthy, weighty topics punctuated conversations,
           Endlessly interesting.
                Concepts were as varied as was the individual.

Always intriguing, sometimes pleading,
    Close bonds formed in these engagements
        Were forged from real life's chains and chances.
           Opening uncharted territories
              Was simply par for his course.

This life was "Beautiful."
    It was floating, flying, above,
        A genuine moment of worship
           Spanning all that was to be endured.
              "It made me forget my pain."

Larger vistas devolved into living landscapes.
    Introductions gave way to fresh instructions.
        Building from without and within,
           Shifting, sparring, sparing, and sharing quantitative
learning and application,
              Images' small miracles suddenly burst onto the
scene.

Seldom would fear inhibit ambition,
Or prevent invigorating, determined, and arresting
exploration.
Unfamiliar territories could startle the novice.
These quests invited full participation.
All who accompanied him knew this.

I miss him greatly.
Support, fun, playfulness,
Competition, composition, adulation,
Questions, and deep, heart-rending discussions,
Though silent now, are not forgotten.

He was family, a friend, a learner, and teacher.
Supporter and inquisitor, he longed for truth.
The softer side too often dwelt 'neath unrelenting pain.
Though severe discomfiture pervaded, it did not
prevent inquiry into deep truths, life-changing and
eternal.
If anything, it made him stronger.

Steadiness longed for solitude, the crying of the soul.
Outside pressures overwhelmed him.
In these times,
Isolation was reverenced,
Distance honored.

He grew in faith.
He worshipped God.
He cherished family.
He honored friends.
His life touched many lives.

Mine was one of them.

In Remembrance of Keith

Mixtures

Separated as oil from water, dilatory, noncommittal, oddly
existing, colliding and complex, shared proclivities confirm,
"There are no solid grounds."
    Heights, lows, fears, and confusion reveal traits of those
    who, on one day stand tall and on other days, shrink
    before the slightest adversity.

Within futility, love's gifts are rare and there is no merry-making.
    Living, dying, blooming, withering, each one stops before
    starting again if a movement's cessation is required.
    It often is.

Special deliveries come not, communication's languages utter
phrasesthatrequireexcessivereinterpretationsbecausethey're
no longer heard.
    Sensibility has vanished.
    There are no raw materials or tools with which to craft a
    structure where truth replaces fear.
    There are no songs that all agree possess lyrics that
    are prescient, timely, needed, respected, honored, and
    obeyed.

Passingfadingcomprehensionsofmost, a few may strive to quell
the tumults from the masses.
    They needn't try too hard.
    "All of this will work," is folly.
    "There shall be no doubt," is false.

Walking well-traversed trails, stumbling is still natural and a
common occurrence.
>Ego-maniacs distance themselves, imposing constrictive
>rules, refusing to hearken, least of all to obey their own
>requirements.
>Adulating screams fill arenas packed with simpletons
>who, for their experiences, actually paid for the privilege.

It is unbelievable.

Suppress the noises from milling throngs who join exclusively to
satiate personally unfilled requirements:
>These fleeting enthusiasts fade quickly when life calls,
>usually the next day.
>On this you can count—without a hint of a doubt.

Regularities of inconsistency boggle deeper minds who
contemplate and participate in never-ending quests for greater
understanding.
>Endeavoring to reconcile what may be irreconcilable
>they grow through trying and learn from striving.
>They will not cease their efforts.

There would be far fewer souls seeking accustomed emotion-
driven experiences if their core existence and accompanying
revelations were real in the first place—authored, authentic, and
accountable— while experiential in heart, soul, mind, emotion,
communication, and touch.
>This is not too much to ask for those unsatisfied with
>meaninglessness.
>The quest is required for those who will only be satisfied
>with more than mediocre, morose, moronic, and unmoving
>mysticism.

More

Graceful fingers melt away aches and pains, relieving the stress
points of guile.
>Discerning, uncovering tears, mending tears of complex
>emotion,
>Unfixed, one yearns for balanced understanding.

Weight paces a presage of impending good deeds, though
temporary.
>Relief, though through living agony, wishes its
>protagonist to suspend the struggle,
>Eradicating cruelty and replacing it with salve.

Once more a touch, whence it comes, spreads joy freely.
>Pervasive and distilling, if affects all.
>Balance washes away impurities; they die.

Desires for stored up penitence let go unessential goads.
>A process disclosed is refreshment won.
>An organ and its pipes resonate, rejoicing.

Come home to this music, this moment, this mood, and its sublime
meditation.

Movement

Worn-out verbiage cannot express breathless descriptions of wonder
>Rising from the unexplainable and unimaginable.
>Bolting away and giving back,
>They practice the essence of life.

Inhaling, exhaling,
>The diaphragm never tires while causes for next breaths endure.
>When shall it rest and, more importantly, how does rejuvenation occur?
>Proportionately, requesting eight hours, the body contributes sixteen.

A miraculous momentum surges and urges, serendipitous.
>Reliving struggles if long over-drawn
>This account will not allow.
>Peaceful rest bids momentum to slow when it must.

Blocked by gluttony's objections,
>An organism's rhythms are constricted.
>Halted, a reassessment is born.
>It realigns quickly.

May it ever be so to interruptive discourses?
>Those pattering displays,
>Interpreted fully,
>Offer little of truth in the matter.

The natural reaction is to let them go.
    Breathe in, breathe out.
    Restrain holding breaths to prove endurance in the
    wrong seasons.
    Conclusive causes speak that rhythms of life are
    yours anyway.

Align with them and live.

One

From the inside, looking out, one is pulled, pushed, shoved, and
stung.
  Confinement breeds confusion and returns frightening
  obliterations.
  Reasoned but unfulfilled love is where this crucible
  dwells.
    Losses raise inaccessible desires as each dawn
    comes anew.

Seize a day or grant its going.
  A choice away,
  No echo returns
    From words not spoken.

A mime, in time, performs your part.
  Instilled relativity is not truth.
  Embrace the dance.
    Then create your own.

In refreshment,
  Breathe anew,
  Lifting arms high
    To purchase heavenly stores.

Sounds, tonal
  But not fixed in aggregate,
  Join in full complement,
    Enraptured, captured, lured.

Completed ere completely needful,
  Charming the competent,
  Benefiting the bearer,
    These reside in reserves of the heart and depths
    of the soul.

Opening

With transitions burned onto their psyche and their capacities
spiked through torment, throngs mingle, plodding along roads
framed by thorn-infested, rough-hewn, and overgrown hedges.
   Collected views, tantalized, complimentary, support the
rejected.
      Fuller spirits, chipped away,
         Swagger and stagger beside bloated clefts.

Tombs of time, their inlaid walls waiting,
   Beckon servitude to linger as scales weigh worth,
   for in time all disintegrate to dust.
      Balance, unachieved, still tries to soften death blows'
      inflicted cuts.
         Unaligned shadows mock the struggle for survival.

Crosses interrupt pervasive perspectives, rewriting them
unnaturally.
   Penciled chapters fade.
      Fattened belligerence burns inside inbred laziness,
         Slipping; too much truth is exposed.

Rescue the fool-hardy if consciousness of condition enlightens
hope.
      Unobserved ignorance, minus ideology's ideals,
         Gathers and clings to the forlorn in choking dust, 'mid
         dank crevices, lethargic.
            An outsider's pleadings to assist them
            go unheeded.

False the impressions these dark edifices portray!
   Prolonged delusions dismiss tolerance as explosive energy
   builds but is expended needlessly.
      Straggly accents defame weakened pleas.
         Sipped, cabernet flows as bodies run the gauntlet.

Futility's efforts mock their courses.
   Authenticity dies in seasons that never gave it birth.
      Green tissues and silly thoughts tender shallow
      conversations.
         Dashed hopes and longevity's denials race toward
         abandonment.

Spaces compartmentalize nothing and reveal everything.

Passion

Obsessed with zeal and jealous appeal,
    Unreasonable expectations provoke obtrusive finger-
pointing.
    Even after tinsel is removed a tree retains its in-
borne majesty.
    Design, destroyed, passes, but the core remains.
    Dead leaves, dried, crushed, and blown become mere
tokens.

Nature exposes intent.
    We shall, too.
    Rites of passage
    Possess bridges that shift
    But do not crumble.

Resilience—like mammoth rocks—
    Resides in place
    Though tested by time and cause.
    Endurance is marked with the priceless and most
important,
    Standing unmoved through faddish fixes, surpassing
trends and meaningless fables.

Generations tell truth.
    History shall not be rewritten.
    Cycles, through decades of unsettled atmospheres,
    Speak of new lives ascending from decay.
    Though decadence's intemperance births tomorrow's
remembrance, redemption still shall come.

Love.
    Spring comes, a part of every year.
    Gently go forth, anew.
    Live and prosper.

Planted

May I, your source of pleasure, be
A servant-master paid or free,
Whose truth presented and returned
Becomes in deed our lesson learned?

The student braces when you try to explain it.
Even plenteous, purer motives centered in repeated receptivity
struggle in the quest.
There are no denials here.
A due process, composed of ends which meaning brings,
Births lonesome subjects in the paragraphs a giver seeks to
complete.

Secrete the gift—its seeds of longing are guarantees of
abundance.
Unfettered contributions will not constrict the contracts of
investments that last beyond themselves.
Laws live, whether accepted, spoken, acted, or not.

Grocery bags and twenty-bills
May not reveal their framer's wills.
A scratched, handwritten note conceals
The true intentions of the deal's
Originator.

Tendered, harvested benefits have reached thousands,
and increase.
Never imagined were any to proffer mere one-to-one returns.

Portion

Deserted and alone, darkness trespasses endless voids, calling
ghost-like shadows to consume what lingers.
    Hearken toward lifting spirits who define superior and
noteworthy places, framing compositions that live.

A counting, a reckoning discloses futures that shall not receive
compensation before their times.
    Savor sure investments, building strong to last.
    Prepare for your tomorrows ere they become your past.

This is no phantom or pantomime.

Film never captures
Slight, fleeting raptures
Where uncounted memories remain,
While presence of beauty
'Mid motions of duty
Bids unruly angers refrain.

Worn from care and homeward-bound,
A lonely soldier wanders 'round
The long-deserted fields of sticks and stones,
Till acceptance of the mastered
Lines a truthful prescience shattered,
Whose commander's spirit craved The Greater Cause.

Deep contentment's tender touch
Engenders views that relish much
Of otherwise condemned behavior's calls,
Where a living while it's dying,
Upon flesh no more relying,
Rather, fastens on foundations from the past,

Where the dogmas are not dictums and its people are not
victims,
Rather, souls with fresh perspectives not yet cast.

In quests for greater meaning,
Understanding that their leaning
Toward truth will break the mold of common threads,
It's a fact that few remember
As apart from fuel an ember
Dies a slow though glowing death in flame's demise,

Where concepts learned from teaching
Are their rules not grasped from reaching,
Where facts of life equate to greater sums,
And rewards received in silence
Are from conflicts won through violence:
These the costs incurred before the ending comes.

Coarse requirements are for creatures who find it difficult, but
possible, to think and act on their own judgments.
This is freedom.

Position

Privately, within cloaked and concealed enthronements of
perceived royalty,
> Where it is presumed no one hears through walls thought
> to be impenetrable,
> Voices can be heard over resounding encumbrances
> If one listens closely enough.

People lend their ears.
> Or, at least, they should.
> Eventually they will.
> Here, utterances and shell-masked laughter are
> rehearsed in dying arias.

From cursory in-dwellings the cries of pent-up emotions emerge.
> Hardened hearts and un-relative thoughts without
> inhibition
> Ascend as if by design, accelerating freely toward silo-ed
> crescendos.
> Will the Fine never come?

Choose.
> Then choose again
> Life's focus points behind and in front of cacophonies,
> Multitudinous phony and restless vibrations.

Criticism's decaying and twice-laid decadences no longer affect
thickening and drying mud.
> Clear water runs o'er tranquil scenes in lapping rivulets.
> These conquer any stone,
> Given sufficient time, agony, and unrelenting motion.

Power

Staged photographs simply do not tell the truth.
>Retouched, as are the beings in the picture, the image is
>the focus.
>Photography may represent no picture of life as it truly
>is, or was.

Behind the lens and before the pose, the one who captures the
shot for the ones for whom it's captured may not be informed
but will surmise.
>Yet, the product hangs, proclaims its lie, as though
>happier times were born before they died.
>How false, how misconstrued and terribly unfortunate
>for the generations who are to come, who may not learn
>this story, but only theirs afresh.

Coping will be their lot.
>Good luck.
>May blessings come.

Beauty does not reside in beholders' scenes.
>Those who gaze upon the truly gorgeous ones
>Misunderstand, somehow, that these sparkle no matter
>how they look or where they live.

Trumped up, they appear to endure beyond a photographer's
click and the memory of the momentary.
>Power-hungry persons portray a stance which is not, to
>convince the ones who have not, that though they will
>acquire naught, the image will not tell.
>Quests for positional significance pale in comparison
>to truths of day-to-day encounters, those places where
>people's lives unfold.

Photographers capture fleeting fancies; these are intruders.
    Audiences anticipate glimpses, and glare.
    Yet, these films are retouched, too, for the portrait
maker's reputation is at stake.

Poured out, these poor folks must only contemplate the "What
if I...," remaining in the unachievable until the dawn of their
departures, where images will be framed with different borders.
    Withered agendas, and those who required them, must
finally cease their calls for faded hopes, fruitless desires,
and unsacred acquisitions.
    The consternation of the undernourished feeds the
insatiable longings of the grossly unfulfilled.

    If you look closer, you will recognize it every time.

Few care, and fewer may acknowledge it, except those who read
the writings and view the photos, pondering them far beyond
mere hasty contemplation,
    Relishing a moment and relating to them from viewpoints
of history,
    Oft quoted, but seldom heeded.

Presumption

Come away from the familiar.
    Chronological misery provisions those who persist in
    ignorance.
    A desire to make room for alternate perspectives
    Calls to fathoms unplumbed.
    Persuasion from trusted sources, to break the molds,
    Questions responses usually offered.

A term may repel unspoken agendas.
    Inaccessible fields reveal landscapes over dismantled
    fences.
    Acceptance, tried and denied, having borne a
    hopelessness aside,
    Meets conditions, but this is no free gift!
    This, in fact, could be nothing more than mere
    manipulation.
    Wise the ones who tell falsity from truism.

Construed, misgivings push power and fall.
    Along with their self-serving trappings they topple into
    shunned places,
    The tiny, foreboding, dirty, and back corners
    Where old formulas, revisited, inflict pain upon forgotten
    opportunities.
    Unfilled commitments, remembered,
    Ask for alternate replies.

        Facades shelter tears.
       Lost ones cannot be rescued
        No matter the degrees of
         Fomented guilt.

         Remember this.

Heaped into tiers,
 A sixth is all, but for some enough, to incite recurring
 delusions.
 But for repose, while being still grows,
 Their faculty shows
 How ridiculous are their conclusions.
 Repulsive experiences of historical significance fix lasting
 indifference.

Barely aware,
 Surface bliss blesses nothing of permanence.
 Migrations invite all manner of interested parties.
 Questions remain unanswered for those who never ask
 them.
 Those who think about nothing more than temporary
 shelters for themselves
 Presume too much.

Pulse

Settling accounts, determined souls, striving to make sense of
the records while reviewing voluminous ledgers, grieve as they
wander through rolling tallies and incorrect totals.
      Awakened from a prior day, comparisons with the past
      fail and compassions falter.
      More desperation is the final toll.

Poured wine of soured grapes tantalizes even the most
discriminating palates from a distance.
      Tastes repel
      As does the smell.

Above the bar, chimes call.
      Quelling transfixed and shattered nerves, they linger.
      But rest is not sure, not yet.

Linked to life, cycled history's lessons reprise their courses
      Until learned ones, reprieved,
      Emerge better for having lived them.

Accepted admonitions grasp unwilling and perishing
parishioners
      Who, while invited to feasts where delectable victuals
      crown knightly tables,
      Never make the Guest List at home.

Pock-markedfloorsnolongerencapsulatedesperateintentions.
      Crusaders retire into unknown hill countries, tied to
      appearances of what could have been.
      Distant memories and hapless dreams give up the ghost
      and perish.

Glassy eyes glisten, longing to reshape epics when viewed
through new prescriptions.
    Merging images, drawn into a rehearsal's preparations
    No longer linger in fears of falling or tears from failing.

Sneering faces, ashamed, turn away.
    Rhythmic sensations, though barely beating, take center
    stage.
    Lights are not extinguished—they never were.

Ready

Facing the grand entry, at home where it belongs,
Conspicuously occupying its place on the stone-carved mantle,
A mighty icon rests, honoring scenes of gracious living and
imaginative giving in former times.

Weary eyes and care-worn ties,
Characters of truth and lies,
Break from repetitious sighs, and
Things.

Eager, through celestial lifting,
Treasured objects go through sifting,
Fading, though a tiny remnant
Clings.

Opened shutters down the hallways
Tell the myriad of small ways
Harmony, when roused, obeys, and
Sings.

Though rebuked, those who prevent progression
are not ashamed.
Hungry for more, they insult and intimidate any who permit them.

Meager ones may strive to live within permutations dreamt,
Or, over time, growing new confidence, they will arise and
conquer, proven real.

Embrace and carry stricken beings into places of renewed
essence,
Into quests of universal passion and pure motive; assist those
who desire more.

Bitter pills are easier to swallow when mixed with sugar and spun
honey.
Healing progresses toward an end and discovers conquests
in the making.

Recorded

Preservation hordes inadequate ideology and fails every time it tries.
Time robs though causation longs for that which shall not be again.

Empty hands beat thinning air.
No one is there to record or recall.

Take it all back?
Try to re-tell it?

These are brothers in a dysfunctional family,
A mother and father leading adversarial siblings who,
As childish adults, re-tear thin fabrics of familial ties, passing,
Passing them to future generations, infecting all.

Upheaval spreads degradation and error,
Fighting self-controlled and cooperative environments.

Contrasted with simpler expectations,
They conquer the resistance with which they do battle.

What of endurance?
Trials, in abiding forms, finalize finishing touches.
Borne on airs of experience, hope, or engagement,
Resilient ones live and thrive, regardless.

Residues are summations of what could have been
Unfinished sentences whose periods have passed
And for which no period will be used

Reflection

Mirror's images pass impressions and pour learned offerings
into willing minds, stewards of memory's treasures.
      These repositories are subject to their owners.

Droplets, borne aloft on passing winds, interrupt sunlit spans,
calling porous grounds to receive their wares.
      These become caretakers of living revelations.

Flowered delicacies hearken to impulses as a hungry person
desires to be filled, whose life, enriched, nourishes others.
      Their consequences endure.

Fleeting, fanciful beauties without constraint bow to the laws
that gave them life.
      Their stories are retold.

Useless restrictions repel the self-controlled.
      These servants are not bound.

Obedience to pleasures reveals the physics they support.
      They mirror essences of their composers.

Undaunted, a truly beautiful one knows her strength and shows
the passersby naked revelations.
      These exist, regardless.

Much like antiquities, aged but ageless, when mined and refined,
      These abide and instruct those who observe and learn.

Waiting for its only chance,
A tiny flicker takes romance
Into a realm of distant dance
And living is renewed.

Rehearsal

A softened contact, though tiny and tentative, pierces old abrasions.
>   Persevering, phalanxes intentioned on moving the mighty
>   May throng the gate and break through.

Surfaces are saturated with an artisan's incongruities.
>   Rough spots smoothed, touched by time, are cajoled and caressed.
>   Enduring truths, destined to dwell in safer lodgings, in another day and time, perhaps, will emerge.

Audiences applaud inference's inspiration.
>   Deed and greed join.
>   It is inevitable.

Perspiration lives in challenge.
>   Impetus to influence is a tedious process few complete.
>   Work the work of spell-binding by doing the deeds.

Benefits befit the searcher and learner, the living, the lover.
>   Rhyme the beatings of the heart and tenderly approach another.
>   Companionship at these levels is thoroughly enjoyed.

Reversed directions morph a fool's desires for shallow engagements.
>   These are the dreams of the damned,
>   Condemning never-realized potentials.

Students, who investigate, sing reprises of deification's songs.
>   These must be sung.
>   They will be, perhaps imperfectly, but with gusto.

Cored essence covers death's wishes and finalizes all.
    A true story lies buried beneath the ruins.
    The apropos of discomforting times turn toward
    alternative and more attractive views.

For those who seek deeper callings,
    Wealth and worth proclaim,
    "Listen, Learn, Live, and Love."

Waves break in the absence of the beach-gone frenzy.
    Discontented conversations spit injustice to offerings,
    But the affect is nil.

Justice wills eternity's experience.
    It will never be bored from trying.
    It will never give up.

Reign

Drifting independently, the droplets fall, missing their marks,
    Bearing little consequence,
        Portending no imminent danger.

Immanent groups coalesce, forming freely.
    They demur to their destinies,
        Waiting.

Banding, branding, racing, and running with the winds,
    Jostled juggling and foaming swell the tides
        As an onslaught's claps of thunder resonate through the
    valleys.

We are reminded how awful and foreboding this solitude is,
    Gliding silently, glowing clusters of light then dark,
        Ominous—

Shared characters in sacred and quiet stories at home—
    Soon will be unleashed when comes the ferocious fray.
        What will the onlookers do?

Unceasing and uncensored, torrential downpours bellow with
belligerence.
    They misbehave, though none can alter their importunity.
    We can only marvel at their powers.

Crafted demands and delicate obstacles are demoralized,
    Shattered to bits on flows of tides aroused from unknown
    quakes,
        Fomenting wrath on distant shores.

Bulwarks tried and found wanting are overcome, obliterated.
    Forces greater than self-reliance have conquered them once
and for all.
    Their expressions of struggle endure but for a
microscopic epoch but are remembered for generations.

Release

Lessons from former times teach eternal truths.
    Who listens to their messages, responding while in youth?
    Do not newcomers of their own volition, learn?
    Violations and validations, re-birthed, thrive and strive in
    infant's lives.
    Cyclical, building cumulatively, wiser ones balance
    incongruities and cooperative activities diverse
    perspectives bring.

Sensations, sensitized, cradle the youngest.
    Abhorring old ways, adolescents fashion what are to
    them new views.
    Amassed limbs reach higher but are cut down,
    Save only those spared by higher authority and willful
    obedience.
    Straight edges interrupt crude curves by movements of
    stirred   imagination.

Original sensibilities argue vehemently.
    Few obey while hosts openly rebel.
    Interests are piqued.
    It doesn't matter.
    Drowned rats emit poison still as do young rattlesnakes.

Rookies play this game.
    So-called fame awaits the winners.
    A concept learned is a stove-taught burn.
    Not to touch or touch with conditions,
    This is perceived truth.

Lie wistfully in experiences of gracious contemplation, satisfied.
    None compare to this.
    None could.
    Enchanted bliss is pure release:
    A formula's living function.

Exploration yearns for more than the status of unfulfilled
dreams.
    As meteor showers set skies ablaze,
    Enveloped lights, flickering,
    Form and streak, fleetingly,
    For a moment thrilling all the senses.

Altered images emerge from old.
    At first, they are unrecognizable.
    Doubts diminish when distant horizon's mists fade away.
    None subdue earnest ones in their quests.
    These fashion history in their present.

Laughable are those who contest the conquests of the ones
    Who desire to exceed, refusing to merely wish upon a
    star.
    Folks who peek beyond their forlorn conditions
    Rise to foreign and forgiven states, asking,
    "Why?" and "Why not?"

Remainder

Silent, carved in marble, a sentinel's speech distills glory,
courage, and belief,
Relating stories of savage struggles.

    Water, wind, weather, wear, and secret warnings
    Remain and
    Rouse the curious.

        They will beyond today.

As stones cry out
    So these speak in tongues and tones
    Unheard but recognized,
    Reciting the unfathomable, "How could they?!"

Bread and sustenance wrenched from unforgiving bounds'
persistence at first condoned then condemned trickling rivers of
sweat from servitude's laborers and those that bid their painful
groans increase.
    Combined within larger, longer images and imaginations,
    Rewound in contemporary interpretations of immense
    tragedy,
    Contemporaryconclusionsareapartofhistoricalaccuracies.

        The struggle lives,
  Enlivened by younger sentinels and soldiers of fortune.

The deceased speak.
    Modern words, composing conflicting re-writes,
    Still reveal entitlements not forgotten and timed to
    invade over souls with,
    "Never again."

Do we pass by and little notice?
    To ignore is to be woefully ignorant.
    Even amid unceasing intensities of foreordained
    consequences,
    A timed journey emerges as do eternal principles.

Bathed in mists, visitors pause, contemplative or confused.
    No separation silences vigilant and resounding voices
    Though historians make havoc of the evidence,
    Prompting and promoting erroneous facts.

They cannot, nor will they ever
  Redo,
    Remake,
      Remold, or
        Remove
          That which ever shall be
         Unresolved
           Unless dealt with.

  Promises of resolution and restitution may reside with you.

Repetitiously

Patterns perform recurring passages,
Nurturing, supporting a composition's impact,
    Molding thoughts,
    Sweeping enduring matters
    Into mementos held close to the breast.
        These engender gratitude from ones previously
        held at arm's length.

Mindful adventurers weigh risks and take them.
An anticipated consummation, in its retelling,
    Unveils priceless treasures to formerly inattentive ones.
    At first feeling,
    Then reeling,
        They are pushed beneath and beyond reality.

Oral tradition lingers as stories unfold and persuade retention,
    Positioned in the mind,
    Expressed as finely hewn diamonds,
    Never fading,
        Brilliantly alive.

Relived visitations comprehend recurrence.
    These attenuate alternating and competing voids,
    Entering without inhibition.
    Treasured once, now, and again, enlightened
    understandings are destined to live,
        As do their tales.

Passing ages deepen comprehensive Truth.
    Longevity is not measured in one generation.
    Aberrant changes invade lives and enter the abodes of
    observers.
    Stronger persons are not adversely affected.
    These mold futures for themselves and their companions.

Reserve

Long ago, preparing what must be, an appropriation, its
attention finessed
    To minute arrangements,
        Secured rooms, spaces, times, and places,
           For these were the required accoutrements.

Success or failure,
      A scene in development,
        Seen under lights of dutiful preparation,
         Shone when its presentation began.

Shall relations bear variances within time-honed and age-
honored truths?
      Why does warbling of an unnatural descant's trills
        Abandon a melody's intricate details,
          Shoving others aside, seeking to exist alone,
         removed, and noticed above the rest?

What is assumed, though wearily borne, is obliterated.
    What is infused heightens resolve.
        The seasoned are invigorated.
         They thrive.

Place settlers move into patterned paces,
     Engaging processes, honoring their predecessors.
       They are supported by those who understand
      responsibility.
         One ties and buffs the other's shoes, making ready
        all.

Requisites for completion and transformations marry.
Combined, they compose fresh stanzas.
These refuse to be marred
When conjoined.

Restitution

Greet the dawn.
    It's overdue, rarely overdone, but daunting.

Simple laborers shed duties as old clothes or keep them as
rewards for servitude.
    Souls toiling in forbidden soils bruise the very hands that
    must remove the stones.

Straight trenches are soon forgotten
    When covered by scraggly surface shrubs.

Doctors prescribe.
    Patients subscribe.

Tombstones inscribed, tell their fates.
    These viewed health sideways.

It never felt quite right.
    Might they have tried other remedies?

Shallow and hollow expectations
    Evolved in queer experimentations.

Glances, prances, dances, romances:
    These are chances that warriors take.

Relative motion careens, remaining in a foreign journey's
devotionals.
    Waning reflections collect in moistened thoughts,
    flowing down in dust-bordered rivulets.

Homeward bound is a bounce,
          Not a rest.

A large and bending bough will break of its own weight if the
mighty one is not cut down
          Before it cracks and rends at its weakest point.

Clip its sinews!
          Dismember from the host a former beautifully adorned
          and admired one.

Death-laded, upon once fertile ground, it dries before your
eyes.
          It must soon be discarded with the residues of other
          trash.

What was sown is yanked and thrown
          When seen to satisfy no more.

Quests and requests bid speakers and listeners consider
opposing ideologies.
          Prophets proclaim that none can be granted fully.

Perhaps nothing shall remain of the encounter.
          Then again, maybe something will.

Sixth and seventh senses
          Live in perceptions of intensely personal realities.

They shove each other purposefully
          To be noticed beyond the ordinary.

Reward

Lemon juice preserves the core
    If for this purpose it is well applied.
    Banning discolorations it spoils an intrusive instrument's
    effects.
    For a time—
    Endurance.

We may not eat what protects what we can.
    It is thus in human endeavor.
    We learn this.
    Tastes and time remind us.
    Others tell our story.

Efforts screened, surrounded by pain,
    Effectuate intentionality.
    Nets and workings of intertwined connections are tied to
    longer ropes, eternal hopes.
    To those who taste and see, to eat is to grow, to learn,
    to know.
    Ties might be severed to achieve greater strength
    in new associations, but we prepare for this.

Natural chemic harmonies balance organic compositions.
    These live another day.
    Shown to dedicated souls, actions are justified.
    Realism is won for one, one more time.
    While demise is retarded, it remains inevitable as motion
    stirs.

Tart is good.
Preserve what you can.
Living is rewarded.

Secure

In spoken and unspoken messages the signs of the times speak
volumes to those who notice.
> Unfiltered and intrusive voices raise decibel levels and
> stubbornly refuse to depart.
> Their roles, played well, compose piercing annoyances
> that bother and berate the attentions of travelers who, in
> periodic solitude, regain strength to live.

Block the intruders.
> Continue former courses.
> Lonesome hearts awaken eager company, refusing
> disinterested companions, minions whose capacities for
> care are measured in mediocrity, who dwell in destitution.

Considered and weighed, waiting no longer for tides to turn,
circumstances beg to be altered by ones whose desires outlive
transient though momentous destruction.
> Shining, their stories are told in song, lyric, dance, and
> poetry.
> Their tales live within vast numbers of tomes whose
> communications, when opened, are devoured by
> knowledge- and wisdom-hungry beings.

Resuscitation room's doors open wide for them.
> Longing ones grasp for more than a little and in excess of
> their contemporaries.
> They will not be refused.

Their enemies appropriate multifarious forms.
  Fortified barriers, strong, forbidding walls, paintings
  on the ceiling, décor adorning halls, mere images, all, are
  formidable foes.
  Speaking truths beyond words and vital signs ne'er
  witnessed by eyes of a machine, these must be seen for
  what they are and for what they are not.

There is more.
  Shall we not venture beyond what we know?
  Shall we not enter places we should go?

Hidden, but longing to be freed, a slate of yearning, a place of
learning, and freedom's earning are won without compromise
despite insurmountable odds.
  The cost of this journey is worth it for brazen discoverers.
  Others are convinced the price is too high.

            Restrictions and ties,
            Half-truths and lies,
            In smiling disguise,
            Restrain one who tries.

    Stemming the mind's contemplations that matter,
    The cruelly insensitive, drowned in their clatter,
        Clutter their places with emptying chatter,
    Contending the former, content with the latter.

Dwell where few have ventured.
  Go willingly into wonder, assured of yourself and
  your mission.
  Herein is life, for the journey is the destination.

Senses

Aesthetic distance repositions desires within winds of challenge
and opportunity.
>Art responds, remakes, and remolds perspectives.
>Arranging itself, it pulsates with efforts to express and
>alter its objects.
>It charms the dances and romances the dancers.

Intensities rise in concerted movements,
>Separated no longer by artificially induced formalities
>Or endangered by threats from native and naive
>impetuosity.
>This is freedom for many.

Ingenuity shapes its cause, and causes its future.
>Expression affects all who take it in.
>Simplicity seeks audiences of intrigued persons
>Who revel in solitudes together as mid a tumult the eye of
>the storm is calm.

Released, a life unburdens its own.
>Beauties unfold into banners of love.
>Beings declare their desires and, burning with passion,
>begin.
>Willing hearts openly breathe scented and refreshing air.

Imagination's senses reopen once blinded eyes.
>Unveiled in their release, spirited ones discern divergent
>dimensions of spirituality and Spirit.
>These are habitats beyond the experiential, yet true to it.
>The unusual becomes usable and enhances life.

Shade

Foreboding canopies, dark with suspicion,
    Relate ancient secrets in the shadows of the mind.
        Phantompantomimesendlesslyrehearseagainstthereal.
        Shadow's glimpses pass furtively beyond
        dispensations.
            Cooler breezes refresh nocturnal dreams.

Music softens,
    Mysteries rise,
        Freedoms fall
            And compromise.

Desperation fails to discharge soiled raiment, remnants of
struggle and remains of life.
    Ancient lore lures the unsuspecting and prevents the
    prudent.
        A ring's timelessness, symbolizing an earlier covenant, is
        exposed in calamity.
            Fallentruthbearsonlyamarkofwhatreallyoccurred.

Pursed lips both frighten and compel.
    Marks on recently traversed roads leave traces of those who
    lost their way and fell.
        Fondly, but foolishly hoping for clarity,
            Plodders push their companions off beaten paths
            and observe them as they tumble into ditches of
            remorse, offering no assistance.

Patterns cannot be read in the gathering smoke of extinguishing
flames.
　　As warmth was denied and brightness stilled, the greedy
　　would smother a seeker's desire.
　　　　Contented souls have long since departed,
　　　　　Leaving wanderers to muse, alone.

Yet, pilgrims, glimpsing flickering lights of the everlasting
through dense and darkened forests, peer intently in a quest for
comprehension.
　　Ground-dwelling, youngsters crane their necks heavenward,
　　　　Wondering at questions that cannot be answered.
　　　　　Important realizations may reveal themselves in these
　　　　　shaded lanes.

Lanky limbs climb where footholds don't exist.
　　A slip is not a fall and a fall is not a failure.
　　　If hurt does not forbid the climbers to continue
　　　　They will strive anew.

If shade beckons relief,
　　Belief follows as do quests for meaning.
　　　Opposing forces arrayed in unknowns' unholy fears
　　　　Can be conquered when seen for their composition.

Others have traveled, passed through, and emerged victorious.
Who relates their stories of striving, struggle, and strength?
　　　Strangers no longer, they live in us.

Shadow

Conversing awkwardly, unfamiliar personalities strain cords of tolerated companionship when the encounters separate and shield the partners.

    Mighty are the seasons of change that overwhelm them, strengths with which they must reconcile whether they agree or not.

    Shining, the sun spots voluminous targets, honing and directing its rays upon all.

    These move, illuminating sights for the floundering and focused, awakening dimmed and mysterious reflections.

Light and darkness, following each other, capture intentionality.

    Earth and time, cooperatively, spread determination over the willing and unwilling alike—none hide; none avoid mounting and continual contributions.

    Plans bow, as do the people who birthed them, to onslaughts of powers beyond their controls, rising above even distant imaginations.

    Desires to disobey or refusals to align with circuitous and sequential operations are of sure and futile consequence to those who argue with The Infinite.

Withering mid tumults and cravings of their own desires, they truly imagine that what they do has more than a remote capacity to alter sovereign courses begun before they were born.

    Frankly, it's laughable.

    It's tragic, too.

    "Pathetic" is the best description.

The shadow's effects, at this instant or the next, are
unobstructed although unknown.
> Enclosures last but for fleeting seconds when
> contrasted with eons of earned receptivity, where
> enduring statutes reside.
> Of what ilk am I, or are you, and the families of men and
> women?
> Purposed along its lengths, inching, graying, seasoned
> and certain, crawling, its pass, overarching and
> consumptive, lingers merely long enough to straddle
> heaven and earth, shifting saddles and trading seats as
> do preset gravitations that move toward eternal rest.

Solitude

Noise, destroying harmony, is burdensome, no matter its source.
Endurance contests its presence when invasions flood
the state, a sporting arena in which one is compelled
to engage and from which driven extrication for the
accosted becomes the goal.
Permeating, vast, and mundane modulations infectiously
interrupt even the most resistant forums.

Hearing an expanding range's sudden pulses pushes persons so
infected to listen longer and pay closer attention to purer tones.
Atmospheres, clogged with unrecognizable pitches,
satiate no one who is mindful of more than merely
mindless audio.
Purpose-lost, non-importance-infused, these pointless
inputs calm sorry and belabored creatures who in
vacuumed states drift meaninglessly, confused.

Impertinently, restless and relentless waves encroach upon
shallow listeners and pass like thunder claps rolling over
unsuspecting and soulfully uninspired and ignorance-laden
landscapes.
Single occurrences multiply.
Predatory, more of them occupy pathways of invasion
and, without invitation, on they come.

If not abated they overload the system and overcome the
strong and silent grids of courteous and thoughtfully enhanced
environments.
Thought-borne plans, though treasured, lose the wealth
of their experiences enjoyed by their former owners.
Sound alterations are not sound after all.

Droning machines cannot replace the gentle and rhythmic though inaudible motions of the delicate bird in flight, whose wings bear it gracefully yet with great strength, fleeting from flower to flower, tower to tower, soaring aloft, overcoming its own weight.

    Breathless, extrapolate this cunning and control.

    Hums of the beating and coursing wings declare, "Life, increase!"

Disturbedstrangers, totingback-breakingandinvasiveburdens, bid these beautiful concentrations cease.

    Few causes encumber the steadfast sufficiently enough to warrant paying attention to needless interruptions to which the masses succumb.

    How many miss so much because they listen to so little!

Surrounded, enveloped, and enraptured by profound, life-altering depths of inward, mysterious yet manifest, soul-entrenched, living-enriched, adventurous, higher-reaching, and universally imaginative thoughts, look to the simple and receive the complex.

    Experiences consume longings in excess of the minute and commonplace.

    Soulful ventures require eons apace with seconds of space when they cry for your focused attention.

Textures

Thin layers fashion comforting rests,
    Places of solitude,
        Inviting,
            Gracious,
                Gentle,
                    Peaceful.

Touch the silence.
    Tears of joy
        Embrace the passionate feeler.
            Running hands offer lingering solace,
                Accepting arms open and welcome tired travelers
                Home to cheer and goodwill.

Bound to destiny,
    Freed to love,
        Impassioned to live,
            Emboldened to go
                Beyond stark valleys,
                    The sojourner accepts this place.

Laughter and pain,
    Losing and gain,
        Wherein resilient truths were captured,
            Produced their stories from withered hands,
                Though hidden
                    Until discovered by simple shepherds.

Texts composed, dies cast, and purposes drawn,
    Plans inked onto ancient scrolls,
        Were predestined to withstand future history's
    onslaughts.
           Wisdom flourished on pages of the dyed and tried.
        Virtuosity reached an eternal present.
      Now we learn from them.

Scribbled lines penned in faded but decipherable handwriting
show promise in records of enduring belief.
    A blank page courts expressions about which writers
   may have issue in this day.
      Write fresh texts.
        Smooth rough edges.
       Savor elegance.
         Create thought.

      Manifold expressions race across this plain,
         Touching the senses,
     Calling the reader to imagination's home.

There Is a Redeemer

There is a Redeemer, Jehovah, Who saves me.
Forgiven, I bow down to worship my Lord.
Amazing compassion that seeks those who wander
And brings them to His light, redeemed and restored.

His love is forever and reaches to lost ones
To buy back the souls who will turn and believe,
Who stand in His presence, forgiven completely,
Unworthy, yet fully accepted, received.

I sing, "Alleluia," give glory and honor
To Jesus, the Savior, who rules everything.
No other can sever this love bond, and never
Shall I cease to praise Him, my God and my King.

Throb

"Put Trash Here."

Behind the far corner of the building a garbage bin, large and
imposing, occupies its space.
Each morning and evening it calls to me,
"Discard your baggage as this day begins."
"Throw off your troubles before you go home."

By what scale is the value of debris determined?
Youth may not understand diverse methods of grading.
There are variant tests and formulas.
Should teachers be compensated solely upon their student's
achievements?

In the heart of an intent a principle rests, inviolate,
though incomprehensible to ignorant and careless ones.
Obedience is proper deference when truth has been revealed.
It does not remove respect from the pure.
Its results are direct and directed.

Few see what cultural mandates belie, the true-to-life precepts
on which they rely.
Patience is required when what is desired is woefully mired in
simple convenience, smacking of instant gratification.
Beauty reaches an apex in stages of lived-out events,
culminating in Now.
This could never have been done before.

Trying, quests call and adventurers respond.
Balanced and gratified, rested for a time, you need to be on
your way.
Perspectives compel the committed to move beyond the plateau
Even when ways are unknown and bodies may grouse and groan
at expending the effort.

Touch

Swirling, sensual, and devotion-laden, tender caresses are
warmly received, aligning with the essence of need and fulfillment
as barren landscapes absorb minute streams.
 Melting swollen bruises, relationship's vacancies are
 re-filled, enriching memories.
 These ebb and flow, rise and fall, depart and come again.

 There is peace.
  There is longing.
   There is future.
   There is faith.

Long walks in cool breezes bid harmonious sounds enfold their
spiritual beings, calling them to release their wearied souls and
enter enchanted and secret places.
 Wondrous, warmed embraces emerge from fingertips
 of those who care.
 Combined with soft enraptured sounds, they compose a
 sweetened air.

 There is serenity.
  There is singing.
   There is truth.
   There is love.

Sands request an ocean's foam to come home and abide.
 Grasps for satisfaction are not heeded by the waves.
 They stay for the briefest time, pausing, but return to
 their origins, consumed.

There is nourishment.
There is growth.
There is harvest.
There is reward.

It is now.
It was then.
These moments obey their own clock.

There is magic.
There is music.
There is harmony.
There is symphony.

It is rising, falling, swelling, sweetly yearning, living and forgiving,
time and timed again.

Trees

Ascending limbs
Proclaim majestic endurance.

Soils in the abyss clutch raw and substantive forms.
Nutrients penetrate earth, permeating dark scenes.
Life and death dwell together, feeding.

Boughs bowed, strain at oncoming winds and, bouncing back,
wave again.
Choosing alternative means and manners, they air
grievances, bend, but don't break.
Discharging energies, they'll live to lean once more.

An edifice's roots resist their bonds and shove aside encaging
debris,
Sanctified to fuller devotion, measured in microcosmic
movements
That bow to no one.

Timid twigs tremble at morning's birth and promise.
Certain ones are crushed, but a number endure.
Stories of survival collect in concentric rings, engraved,
timed, and cherished by those who read them.

Scene and season, toil and tumult in cycles bound, transcend
grit and conquer those who would destroy them.
'Tis just.
The living shall not be prevented.

One always remains.
>Until severed at its core, even then, in fancied lore, a tenant of universal being offers a tiny tentacle to test the winds, waters, and waves, wondering and gaping, grasping at its awakened existence.
>Nourished and maturing, it welcomes winged creatures that soar, praising, feeding, breeding gatherings, evincing exhortation's throaty utterances for all to hear.

>>Endurance-raised and stalwart bulbs,
>>Alive in nature's realm,
>>Though broken, bud, then bloom and burst
>>And none shall overwhelm.

Time is on their side.
>Remote, uninterested, hasty glances, tiny prances, and measured stances mark the passing of disintegrated and ignorant hordes.
>They move as though promised tomorrows will arrive for any who have judged beauty worthy of no attention today.

Pause, ponder.
>Wonder, wander.
>These miracles are nearly incomprehensible.

You are called to embrace an introspective and august Presence.
>You, whose regal liege reflects the past within the present, who presages passages up, out, in, and down, who plans and purposes to live and love, shall learn these are your destinations.
>They may be your destinies as well.

Turned

Arching boldly, arcing toward rising prominences,
   Lightening rends and traverses a midnight's skies,
      Wherein a solitary orb, wandering 'mid endless and
      barren voids,
         Shrieks its eminence, demanding worship.
          Sightseers may claim possession of this
         display
            But only in their minds.

Tell a mountain it shall be moved.
    Proclaim to starving masses that crops will soon appear.
      Steer down-trodden souls on pathways of improving
      fortunes.
         Convince casual observers that all will yet be well.
         Some are amazed but remain unchanged.
           Others who hearken are released from chains.

Most interpret living within views of entitlement,
    Consumed by gluttony and personal greed.
      For the few, comfort is not the object but neither is
      complaining.
         Longings for fulfilled appetites shall not be
         satisfied
          But by turnings of seasons, God-instilled.
            These shall not be controlled by human
            mechanism.

Coverings remain until revelations,
    Perhaps not genteel,
      More like unencumbered revolutions,
         Revel in unadulterated truth
         As it becomes known.
           Cooperation with rhythms brings life.

Men recoil when weakened by their small statures.
Beyond appearances, full depths are released.
Universal callings, languishing in the unspoken,
When gone, are deceased.
When ignored, silence deafens reality.
The wait mounts.

Discovered opportunity asks for one to seize its coming.

Twenty

Numbered mile markers tick off redundant, lifeless stems, wired together and fading toward distant horizons.
> Strewn, strung, and lonesome paths wander, seeking an endlessnothing, spreadingwebbedandwindingnetworks across deserted desert landscapes.
> They bore us.

But they live, too.
> Our ignorance does not prevent their presence or purpose, though unseen, unheard, and rarely noticed. When terminus and sources touch, they count as they are counted.

Hopeful youth drives and sleeps in excess.
> Mirages of glistening patchwork play and tease untrained eyes.
> They fashion respite in distant pictures, but these are void of life.

Wishes for fewer dissolution-pieces evade and evoke non-events.
> Toilsome futures auction their hopes of another year's passing to the highest bidders.
> Closure aligns with perspective and communication paths pass quickly from the mind as markers diminish and attentions are drawn to more enticing realities.

Shattered motives, dirty and dusty from parched winds and dried earth, find fertile oases.
> Surging with energy, producing green foliage, they evolve into vistas of refreshment.
> The desert, and the deserted ones, bloom and boom.

Two

Alone is revered.
> Isolation's winds warm or chill when solitude occupies the central throne.
> Seasons request recompense when more than one distillation occurs simultaneously.

Inner motives and their inquisitive minds rehearse and review the conditions of quiet complexity.
> Contented members invite communion.
> Artificial limits dissolve simply away.

Expressions repressed but compressed no longer, rise in anticipation of at least a hearing.
> Insufficient time, the oft-used excuse, urges reclusive meanings to remain in their dreams.
> Full recognition, only, sets souls truly free.

One prepares, another performs.
> Capacity holds personal preferences close.
> Prisons do likewise.

The desires of one envelop what is required of two.
> Too, feudal repetitions dim and dull the senses, prompting the sullen and complacent to continue in tedium.
> Framed responses make short work of grievances and a simpleton's silly offerings.

Once, then twice, conflicts usher the willing and wanting down lengthening aisles.
> Dew lingers but for a moment.
> Heatevaporatesminisculedropletsunless,underclouds, they collect and combine, fomenting mightily laden streams.

Unquenched

Energies flex, fly, and flourish toward the nub.
    Undulating and unrealistically undaunted, the destined
    and desperate,
    Paired within bonds of trust,
    Shield their timidity, gulp and grasp,
    Holding on, white-knuckled, to un-relinquishing toils,
    Prerequisites to rest so-called, meticulously searching
    for: Why.

Trusted instincts play tricks and drive,
    Themselves driven from within and without by melodious
    flutes' risings and fallings,
    Passing cesspools and oases, receiving mixed messages,
    Unearthed in shaded coverings while rampaging
    confluent streams.
    These foment grief and yearn for life within
    disenchantedsoulsabidinginlaissez-faireenvironments.

Ceased fortunes die slowly, struggling in their demise.
    Re-flexed, muscles want to feel the goading of the good.
    The rush at the end of exertion is worth its sweat
    and pain.
    Blood flow is restored in limbs extended fully.
    Continuance groans and clasps at all who strive beyond
    inconvenience.
    Yours is to not give in.

Views

Anthropological urges lean on ancient understandings.
Unraveling confusions of present intentions, they mark their
time and make their mark.

Up then, down and now then, it's an opportunity for you, then.
As North meets South and East greets West so souls untried
will face this test.

Bore through the familiar and expected with an auger of driven
noncompliance.
Find a greater Why.

Circumstances and obligations request simplicity but dwell in
conflict.
These have no choice in their struggles, other than submission
to nature's laws.

Simple positioning, divided then united, plots a condign journey
all must undertake.
It's been cramped in here.

Belief sprouts assurance.
Weather-beaten, it perseveres.

Flows and flights mount together.
They long to live in symbiotic relationship.

Chords resonate for listeners who allow permutations of original
stanzas.
Hearing like this is rare.

Hearts and hands of inquisitive minds probe the uncharted and experiential.
Guidance from one who knows makes this journey bearable.

The planted one lives.
It procreates its own when in fertilized soil its roots are firmly set.

Vista

Estrangement possesses special appeal for one unfulfilled in
unfamiliar crowds, who, by decree, was alienated from
The Family.
    Defiantly, its membership prided itself in self-proclaimed,
    boisterous superiorities.
    Perhaps gifted in degrees, nothing was granted that was
    not earned.

Outcast, a black sheep wastes no time expending vitalized
energies to mold isolation if necessary.
    He is inspired in his deepest being to become all he was
    meant to be, recognized or not.
    For them, it is a differing point of view and an
    argumentative one—it is conflict where one lives and the
    other dies and is buried in their rut, his grave.

Blurred images creep across old lenses misaligned or marred.
    These require remedies if sight is to be
    restored.
    Sharpened vistas reveal fresh views when new
    prescriptions replace old.

Wine, as old as the bottle it's in, demands no allegiance from its
vessel after all.
    Appeasement, standing tall and ruling arrogantly, fades
    but not soon enough.
    A flower is not its fragile self when pressed.

Transience crawls and sniffs for add-ons.
    Bended knees wear sore.
    Their ligaments break if not lubricated from within.

Perspectives call on behalf of permanence, embracing healing
properties.
    Oils deftly applied purify tendons beneath the surface
    thoughdispensedthroughseverestrugglesfromoutsidein.
    Waning, a lonely one tries to reach beyond conditioned
    malaise though nourishing refreshments reside in
    remembrances.

Learning, if it ever lived, occurred long ago.
    Restlessness stirs in the ash heaps of suppressed
    dysfunction and neglect.
    Compositions muster mighty efforts to bring clarity from
    sources they don't even recognize.

Reality beckons.
    A lingering stance, an alternative path—
    Both await one who refuses contentment beneath
    unfulfilled potential.

Warmth

Tightly wrapped blankets enfold the extremities,
    Warming, surrounding the body on cold, gray, and
    forlorn days.

A being basks, secure, dwelling in imagined places of rapture
and none too soon,
    To live, to leave, to learn, to cleave, and turn another's
    drying leaves; means seize the old, the dried and crushed,
    and willfully discard them.

Cravings, unsettled in uneven tides, awaken dulled senses to
textures and surprising new information
    Where colors dwarf rainbows and shatter golden cisterns
    of unachievable dreams.

Released energy, rising solicitations, emboldened presences,
and calmed silences
    Share similar, if not identical still, small voices.

Whispers of gentle winds pass softly.
    Only coos are heard.

Delicate winged creatures, appearing to be unaffected by
torment and tumult, teach us strength.
    Were we to endure as the smallest of these, beyond the
    cold, what would be our destinies?

Mornings break, peering through tallest shrubs and darkened folds.

    Wispy clouds, intersecting filter-less skies, hazy in blue-green firmaments, forming fragments of the supposed, swagger lazily, remolding and reshaping their personalities.

Sun's rays enliven laughter, reliving Reason's causes.

    Braced, the windows of the mind respond to pervasive winds of truth coming unheeded, uninvited, and impetuously, but welcomed by an earnest seeker. Sons and daughters in their Father's image, facing heavenward, waiting, anticipating, longing for glimpses of the beyond, chance to join a chorus of harmonies blended where bountiful, cozy, and delighted comforts are the marks and makers of homes.

Whole

Cosmiccomicscomminglequests,honingskills,takingtheirspills,
Rising to try again.

Naive people laugh.

Others, intrigued at a war of worlds and words,
endeavor to understand and respond.
Seen from various perspectives, interpretations embrace then
rearticulate mounting desires.

Grains of wheat, of rye, and soy,
Harvests reaped for girl or boy,
Gifts of life and growth and spoil,
Spell their cycles with the soil.

Nexus.

Unsheathed blades, pins of light,
Shared, are spared from no one.
Cast, dispersed, they soon dissolve,
Absorbed in life, to grow one.

Cause the light in wash or streak
To shine upon the fruit you seek.
Operate in truth, ordained.
Crops, in time, will be obtained.

Let wanderings from paths of calling be set aside.
Remain where you are if where you are is home.

Worlds in view will come to you; on this rest, unmolested.
Strength is born in these encounters, though severely tested.

Winding

Unruly creases are pressed to compel unanimity.
    Unwelcome heat requires these folds
        Be pushed toward purposed strength
            Their masters christen "Beautiful."

Through winding cracks and blackened caves
    Magma flows in molten waves.
        Overflowing, meandering, dissolving objections,
          It chooses the paths for its streams to follow.

Wounds, bandaged and wound
    Nearly to constriction,
        Restore themselves over time
          Into enduring realms of youthful resolve.

Therapeutic pressure points will that winding's rests renew the
weary.
    Natural environments,
        Clothed in mystique and merriment,
          Contradict tepid form's moldy, stale, and dying
          formulas.

Canals wend their courses
    As coarse goads etch tracks on smoother stones
        Upon which all who take this trip shall tread.
          There is no running here.

Climbers, convinced the journey brings unrequited joy,
    Approach rugged, rocky mountains to climb them.
        Were surfaces smooth,
          These could not be ascended.

Winding in a single line,
The pilgrims and their sage,
Continue quests for living truths
And write them to their page.

These recount perennial stories
Of those who've gone before.
History's "yes," time-honored notions,
Demands its worth in rhyming motions.
Birthing timely motivations they move
adherents toward destiny's closure.

Juxtapose one another, wound and wind.

Terminus

Knowledge

Knowledge is information received and retained, regardless of sources, whether true or false. Seeking and acquiring knowledge includes testing its veracity and endurance.

What one person knows seldom constitutes information possessed by another. Acquiring knowledge, while often a shared exercise, becomes an individual's enterprise.

What one believes to be true, or not, is proven on the basis of education, experimentation, and experience. Verification comes to each in his or her own ways.

How great is your desire to learn more, about what, and why? How eager are you to grow as a student? How often do you test what you have learned to assure its truthfulness?

Receiving information is a life-long engagement. While many pursue education aggressively, challenging concepts and their authors, others appear to be content with embracing teachings from persons they presume to trust. Numerous people accept proclamations from an instructor, whether qualified or not, on the basis of the teacher's title, station, education, personality, persuasiveness, or experience. These students adhere to perception and reception which evolve into their reality, but fail to realize that what they have learned may or may not constitute verifiable truth.

Acquisition of knowledge is too often confined within walls of third party declaration and interpretation. The responsibility of the seeking person who wants to know *more* is to pursue truth aggressively in individual ways. Methods certainly may include hearing what a teacher proclaims as truth, but possibly should not be limited to it.

Life's counsel is this: Another person's conclusions may become your own when you have investigated the facts and merits diligently, sifted ideas from multiple sources, and reasoned and weighed the worth of multiple concepts and positions. Upon these form initial opinions and final conclusions.

Strong and dedicated efforts of personal discovery contribute to a student's health and well-being. If you are one who learns and sifts information as part of ongoing efforts to arrive at truth, you will, as part of due diligence, decide what to retain or discard. Consider what is most important and why. Evaluate reasons behind conclusions and proof-test them against experience, faith systems, and lasting principles.

Seek information from diverse sources. Life will be richer for the quests of knowledge you undertake as parts of your desires to learn and grow.

Wisdom

Wisdom is a state of comprehension of how to best utilize and apply knowledge within real life engagements.

The person who seeks wisdom studies, validates, and decides motives, methods, and expectations of results. Wisdom looks carefully at opportunities of application and chooses when, how, why, and by whom knowledge will be activated through words and deeds.

Seeking wisdom requires thoughtful contemplation. In this state opportunities and options are weighed carefully. Wisdom considers whether information and corresponding activity will produce benefit or detriment. Possessing knowledge merits little and profits less unless what is known is skillfully used for positive and regenerating impact.

Many possess knowledge and don't use it wisely. Ask yourself:

1. What makes up best uses of what I know?
2. How do I impart and apply information?
3. What are my standards of engagement and application?

Practiced truth in daily living grows positive results when knowledge serves others, uplifts worthwhile causes, holds ethics high, and stands for the right regardless of circumstances.

Wisdom considers timing in assimilating, disseminating, and applying truth. There are right, and alternatively, inopportune moments to gain and apply knowledge into any circumstance and environment. Choose your opportunities well.

Knowledge and Wisdom work well when they work together. Don't separate them.

Action

Action defined: deeds, behavioral changes, and movements of persons in time and place. Action, simply, is doing something—not just pondering it.

Many falter because they fail to move beyond concept to movement. Unless one acts, ideas remain as thoughts, and life is unchanged.

One participates in a process of health when knowledge applied wisely becomes what one does. Nothing concrete is accomplished by merely thinking about what could be. Potential for positive life change remains potential—until a person acts.

Consider these action questions and your answers to them:
1. What roles will you play?
2. When will you begin?
3. How strong are your desires to continue though faced with odds, objections, and crises?
4. What are the expected results of your endeavors?
5. How will others know you are fully engaged?
6. How will what you accomplish affect those you touch?
7. How will you correct errors?
8. How will you celebrate successes?

Destiny

The conclusion of the matter is this: Knowledge, wisdom, and action form a continuum of existence and exercise that produces consequences. Consequences, whether good or bad, are sure.

Destiny is a state of evidence where lessons and actions are evaluated from history's perspectives, and where degrees of effectiveness are weighed. Good or bad, healthy or diseased, results will be consistent with truth or, in the balance, found wanting.

Destiny is a condition created from the start of a process and throughout its term. Acquiring information, understanding how to use it, acting upon it, and evaluating results compose pieces of holistic experience and maturity. Conclusions are found within the processes and remain in the results.

One's destiny may be lofty and known by thousands. Or destiny may be private, revealed to a few. Regardless, it is lived by its originator and remembered by those who observe and receive the effects of prior choices.

Your destiny begins with each moment you learn, think about, and act upon ideas. Processes are cumulative. Consider: What destiny are you building, why, and for whom?

Go From the Night comprises journeys of thought and meditations on life. The poetry and prose explore and question characteristics of human condition and endeavor. The reader's beliefs, sources of stimulation, means of expression, and methods of life application become proof points of acquired knowledge, inspired wisdom, required action, and aspired destiny.

Who you are, what you know, how your goals are achieved, and why, are vital considerations. Discovering and living the answers to lofty questions such as these demand perseverance for the student and teacher, the follower and leader.

Much is at stake. Desires born from within form legacies observed from without. You and those you touch are the beneficiaries.

Greatest Song Among Men

Music by Glen Aubrey

Greatest Song Among Men

There Is a Redeemer

Music by Glen Aubrey

Acknowledgements

Family, friends, and acquaintances are treasures. I have learned valuable truths from persons who have impacted, influenced, and invested in my life.

Contributors have taught alone or in groups. Their fields of instruction have resided within circles of philosophy, art, faith, culture, government, industry, education, and life-experience.

A complete list of these contributors is endless because it continues to expand. Teachers include historical figures I admire and study as well as life contemporaries, some of whom are deceased. All of them have made indelible marks on me regardless of whether agreement exists on all facets of their offerings.

Those recorded here are presented in chronological order, corresponding to the times when I began to receive their contributions. I am profoundly grateful for their instruction, example, and modeling.

Bud and Zela Aubrey
Joan (Aubrey) Longworth-Watterson
Edna Lewerenz
Dale Changnon
Dr. Hoover
Henrietta Mears
Mrs. Alling
Lawrence Welk
Christopher Longworth
Lloyd C. Douglas (*Dr. Hudson's Secret Journal*)

Mary Smith
Abraham Lincoln, the study of whose life began when
Mary Smith recommended a book by Stefan Lorant,
Lincoln—A Picture Story of His Life
Richard Plum
Jenkin Lloyd Jones (*Who Is Tampering with the Soul of America?*)
Jeff Brown
Don Williams
Vernon Lintvedt
Andrae´ Crouch
Don Hubler
Orval Butcher
Jimmy Johnson
Optimist International
Lions International
Otis Skillings
Lee Carroll
R.W. Stringfield
Ken Bible
Henry Mancini (*Sounds and Scores*)
Judy Green
Ron Compton
Derric Johnson (Db #11)
Bill McCumber
E. Stanley Jones (*The Word Became Flesh*)
Bob Hempy
Paul Hontz
Marjorie Sampson
George Gregg
Jerry Jay
Verdel Sorenson
Joe Lubinsky
Vern Larson

Ken Overstreet
Cindy (Zeissler) Aubrey
Calvin and Olive Zeissler
Don Norville
Max DePree (*Leadership Is an Art*)
Carol LeBeau and Tom Hamilton
Walt Ekard
Paul and Sheryl Russell
Rotary International
Heather (Aubrey) Hoffman
Justin Aubrey
Chelsey Elaine
Gary Gonzales
Steve Duff
Scott Coyle
Rachel (Newhall) Pinney
Linda (Sacco) Todd
Walter and June Ekard
Pete Smith
Jack Armstrong
Rick Fleming
Jeff Goble
Keith Koellish
David Hopkins
Rick Hicks
Larry Crabb
Norm Wright
Mike Sollom
Howard Hendricks
Bill Cantos
John Stothers
Bill Bourne
Larry McNamer

James Patton
Nancy Beach
Bill Hybels
Neil Hoffman
Paule-Nora Lessard
Sadie Rose
Jack Elwood
Mark Larson
Doug Gadker
David Fisher
Suzanne Shaw
Katherine Michaud
Michael McLendon
Rick Perrotta
Doug Kirk
Wade Tanksley
James McGowan
Russell Ingledew
Traci Tateyama
Jerald Coleman
Tyler Deyling
Jenafer (Deyling) Aubrey
President and Mrs. George W. Bush
Jim Garlow
Jordan Peck
Dan de la Isla
Mary Walker
Terry Givens
Alisa Edwards
Michell Cook
Jim Standiford

The Author

Glen Aubrey is President and CEO of Creative Team Resources Group, Inc. (CTRG), www.ctrg.com. He is an author, business consultant, leadership trainer, conference speaker, professional musician, music writer and orchestrator, and poet. He has authored *Leadership Is—How to Build Your Legacy, Industrial Strength Solutions Build Successful Work Teams!, Core Teams Work Their Principles and Practices, Growing Core Teams, Core Team Impact!, Go From the Night, Arranging Notes, L.E.A.D.—Learning, Education, Action, Destiny,* and *Lincoln, Leadership and Gettysburg.*

You are invited to visit these websites:
www.ctrg.com
www.CreativeTeamPublishing.com
www.LeadershipIs.com
www.IndustrialStrengthSolutions.com
www.CoreTeamsWork.com
www.Lincoln-Leadership-Gettysburg.com
www.GoFromTheNight.com
www.Lead52.com
www.glenaubrey.com

The Publisher

Creative Team Publishing (CTP) is a division of Creative Team Resources Group, Inc. (CTRG, www.ctrg.com). CTP was formed in 2007 to publish and distribute business and team development, leadership training, and poetry books, as well as literature of inspiration, insight, human achievement, and positive general interest.

The company's commitment is to make high quality literature available and engage in excellence throughout the process of publication. Customer satisfaction is a top priority. Because CTP practices due diligence in selecting which books it will publish, CTP chooses to work with customers who meet a qualified standard of literary competence and uplifting content.

CTP is a fee-for-service publisher. Products offered include the following:

Pre-Press
1. Editing
2. Proofing
3. Revision
4. Typesetting
5. Four Color Cover Design
6. ISBN
7. Print Set-up

Post-Press
1. Product supply
2. Press releases

Contact Creative Team Publishing. Please visit our company website, www.CreativeTeamPublishing.com, for information. We look forward to reviewing your literary creation.

Products

Books and Curriculum by Glen Aubrey
Available through Creative Team Resources Group, Inc.
Online Store
www.ctrg.com

Leadership Is— How to Build Your Legacy

Industrial Strength Solutions Build Successful Work Teams!

Core Teams Work Their Principles and Practices

Lincoln, Leadership and Gettysburg

Go From the Night

L.E.A.D.—Learning, Education, Action, Destiny

Growing Core Teams

Core Team Impact!

Arranging Notes

Music CD Recordings by Glen Aubrey
Available through Creative Team Resources Group, Inc.
Online Store
www.ctrg.com

Beautiful, A Symphonic Experience
Music by Lindamarie Todd and Glen Aubrey

Born Is the King
Christmas Keyboard Reflections
Piano solos

The Custom Album
Piano Solos by Glen Aubrey

Go From the Night Meditation
Glen Aubrey, Solo Piano
Pat Kelley, Guitars
Go From the Night Selected Readings

Meditation
Glen Aubrey, Solo Piano
Pat Kelley, Guitars

Reflecting Hymn
The Rock Album
Piano solos

What Child Is This
Glen Aubrey, Solo Piano

Deeper centers of your will
Consider choices, good or ill.
Aligning with eternal laws
Shall right the wrongs, forgive the flaws.

Mighty those
Who shall oppose
The fearsome foes
One overthrows.

Instilled desires for learning more
Knock hard upon a bolted door.
But open minds and purposed hearts
Embrace what living truth imparts.

9 780979 735813